Equity Crowdfunding

The Complete Guide For Startups & Growing Companies

Nathan Rose

Foreword by Ronald Kleverlaan

© Stonepine Publishing

Third Edition, 2020

Books By Nathan Rose

Equity Crowdfunding (2016):

Equity crowdfunding is a fresh new alternative to venture capital. Startups and growing companies can raise millions of dollars through offering shares to members of the public, while gaining huge publicity at the same time. *Equity Crowdfunding* shows how to use this exciting new fundraising method, featuring contributions and case studies from around the globe.

Chess Opening Names (2017):

Players everywhere know the names of the chess openings, but far fewer know the incredible back stories behind them. Why is the "Sicilian Defense" associated with a Mediterranean Island? Who is the "Staunton Gambit" named after? *Chess Opening Names* is a book which any chess fan will enjoy, no matter their level of ability. Prepare to be surprised, amazed, amused, and informed.

The Crypto Intro (2018):

"Crypto" includes Bitcoin, Ethereum, Litecoin, and hundreds of other digital cryptographic assets. They are borderless, offer universal access, and are free from gatekeepers, central authorities and middlemen. *The Crypto Intro* is the ultimate guide to understanding crypto and getting started, with no prior knowledge assumed.

Rewards Crowdfunding (2019):

Rewards crowdfunding can be used to validate project ideas, build an audience, and raise the necessary cash to get off the ground. _Rewards Crowdfunding_ is the step-by-step playbook for creators intending to launch a campaign of their own. Learn the best strategies from two dozen successful creators, and the world's leading crowdfunding launch agencies.

Contents

Books By Nathan Rose..2

Contents...5

About The Author..8

Foreword: Ronald Kleverlaan..10

Introduction...14

Chapter 1: The Basics..22

    What Is Equity Crowdfunding?...................................23

    How Does It Work?..25

    Which Companies Can Use It?....................................30

    What Is New?...36

    What Are The Rules?..39

    Investor Motivations...41

Chapter 2: Is Equity Crowdfunding Right For You?..................48

    Rethinking Your Need For Capital...............................49

    Fundraising Alternatives.......................................53

    Rewards Crowdfunding Comparison................................59

    Financial Investor Comparison..................................63

    Fees...71

Chapter 3: Structuring Considerations.............................77

Setting The Minimum Investment Amount.......................77

Direct vs. Nominee Shareholding................................80

Private Offer vs. Public Offer....................................83

Prospectus Offer vs. Reduced Disclosure Offer.................85

Types Of Shares..86

International Access..89

The "White Label" Option...90

Should You Use An Agency?......................................92

Chapter 4: Evaluating The Platforms...............................96

Chapter 5: Pitching To The Platforms.............................111

The Truth About Curation.......................................113

Explain Your Business...117

Display Your Credibility...118

Financial Modeling...120

Target Amount To Raise...123

Valuation..125

Show Your Investors...131

Red Flags..132

Chapter 6: Preparing For Your Campaign........................138

General Timeline Of An Offer....................................139

The Value Of A Lead Investor....................................143

What If You Can't Get A Lead Investor?........................146

Writing Your Information Memorandum.........................150

The Lawyer's Role..153

Chapter 7: Marketing...158

    Tactics To Get Attention And Money....................160

    Pre-Launch Marketing Checklist.........................176

Chapter 8: During The Campaign....................177

    The Necessity of Momentum.............................178

    Supporting Your Campaign Post-Launch...........185

    Panic Stations: What If Your Offer Is Failing?.....189

Chapter 9: After The Campaign......................196

    Communication..197

    Delivering on Expectations................................199

    Your Next Round..199

    The Exit...200

    What If Your Offer Failed?.................................202

Conclusion... 207

    Why Equity Crowdfunding Matters....................207

    Parting Thoughts From The Experts....................212

One Last Thing.. 220

Sample Chapter: Rewards Crowdfunding...........221

Acknowledgments..234

Copyright & Disclaimer..................................237

About The Author

Nathan Rose
www.nathanrose.me
contact@nathanrose.me

During my days as an investment banker, the most enjoyable clients to work with were, by far, the early-stage companies going through initial public offerings.

Equity crowdfunding has many strong parallels with early-stage initial public offerings, so when I saw the emergence of this exciting new financing innovation, it was the perfect fit for my interests and skill set.

This book grew out of a desire to provide readers with the tools and advice required to succeed. I traveled extensively to meet the leaders in equity crowdfunding, and interviewed company founders who have already achieved success with this exciting new development in early-stage finance.

Apart from this book, I offer several ways to help founders achieve their growth and funding goals.

- **Free Resources:** There are a host of extra resources to download to get the most out of this book. If you haven't already, I highly recommend heading over to **www.nathanrose.me/equity** to download them, free of charge. You will find a template for making a pitch deck, a checklist for forming your marketing plan, a set of criteria for comparing platforms with each other, in-depth recorded interviews, and much more.

- **One-On-One Strategy Consulting:** I can provide an assessment of the suitability of your project for equity crowdfunding, direct you to the exact platform that will suit your objectives, advise on your marketing strategy, and help hone your pitch to investors. Professional advisors (such as accountants or lawyers), can also receive my guidance regarding what equity crowdfunding can do for their clients. Let's find a time to chat. Send an email to **contact@nathanrose.me** and I'll be in touch.

- **Workshops / Keynote Speaking:** I have written extensively about crypto, crowdfunding, early-stage ventures, and fintech. Financial institutions, co-working spaces, start-up hubs, incubators, and accelerators can have me run a workshop or appear as a keynote speaker. For more information, please e-mail: **contact@nathanrose.me**

Foreword: Ronald Kleverlaan

There are fundamental changes happening within equity finance.

The industry as we know it is currently fragmented, with various institutional investors, venture capital firms, business angel networks, and stock exchanges all targeting different niches. There are many barriers in place for investors and organizations which prevent or discourage the efficient allocation of capital.

In the next decade, it will be transformed into a more inclusive industry, where a much wider range of organizations will be able to raise equity funding and where a much wider range of investors will be able to participate at an earlier stage. Equity crowdfunding has a huge part to play in this.

The growth of equity crowdfunding has been nothing short of phenomenal. It is hard to believe that it was only in 2010 that the first equity crowdfunding platforms started, given that it has since grown to be responsible for approximately US$2 billion in funding in 2015, according to Cambridge University. Furthermore, the industry is almost doubling in size every year.

Startups and growing companies will use equity crowdfunding to raise money and, just as importantly, to connect with their stakeholders. They can then use their investors for improving their business, marketing, and for forming other relationships with the help and knowledge of their network.

The equity crowdfunding market is very diverse. We at CrowdfundingHub have seen the significant growth first-hand, throughout Europe especially. In the United Kingdom, the industry is flourishing with platforms raising hundreds of millions of pounds every year, including dozens of campaigns raising more than a million pounds. In the rest of Europe, several countries are seeing annual markets of €10 - 20 million and higher, with the expectations it will grow quickly to several hundred million euro in the next few years.

We also see many places where equity crowdfunding has not started at all, or is very immature. For regulators, investors, and entrepreneurs, it is important to read the examples and insights in this book to learn why it is so important to support the equity crowdfunding industry in their own country.

One reason equity crowdfunding has not yet developed in some places is a lack of regulation. Equity crowdfunding is not always allowed in all countries, or is very much restricted. In 2016 we saw more countries relax their stance and embrace the opportunities that equity crowdfunding allows – including in the United States with Title III equity crowdfunding commencing.

Back here in Europe, there is a strong push for additional equity financing for companies and innovative projects. Signs are that the European Commission is in favor of promoting equity financing for small and medium enterprises, and specifically equity crowdfunding, in the coming years, through initiatives like the Capital Markets Union.

Equity crowdfunding provides investors with a new asset class to participate in – often higher risk projects with a higher potential return. These include fast-growing tech companies, and also local businesses. Previously, it was too complicated and expensive to gain small investors in such projects, but by providing an online infrastructure and clear regulation, it has now become practical.

Personally, I am a very strong supporter of equity crowdfunding. Instead of a few business angels or venture capitalists, it can be used to build a strong network of supporters and fans who all own a small part of the company. And for investors, equity crowdfunding creates the possibility for them to spread their risk over many more investments.

Managing and communicating with all these micro-owners will create additional challenges, but also opportunities. It is therefore crucial to understand the real motivations of the investors. Most likely, these micro-owners will be able to help the entrepreneur by promoting the company, and to help improve the product or service through the feedback they give. This will create a new form of investor relations, which I like to call "Crowd Relations". When entrepreneurs implement Crowd Relations in the correct way, their micro-owners will be some of their most loyal and supportive fans.

Done properly, companies can grow very fast by using equity crowdfunding. So why is this industry not growing even faster?

At CrowdfundingHub, our observation is that there is a pervasive lack of understanding among regulators, investors, and especially among entrepreneurs and their financial advisors about the potential for equity crowdfunding.

Because equity crowdfunding is still very young, it is important to look globally for good case studies of successful ways to attract funding, and to learn how to communicate and work with these new shareholders. With 20 successful campaigns surveyed, along with input from the biggest equity crowdfunding platforms and interviews with the most prominent experts at the forefront of the space, this book does just that.

Entrepreneurs should not just learn the proper way to prepare their crowdfunding campaign, but must also ensure their company is ready to work as a crowd company. Crowd companies will be more resilient and more capable of adjusting their business to changes happening in their industry.

I'm sure this book will provide the necessary inspiration for your own campaign, and beyond.

Ronald Kleverlaan, September 2016

Founder of CrowdfundingHub, the European Expertise Centre for Alternative Finance and Community Finance

Co-Founder of the European Crowdfunding Network

Advisor on Alternative Finance to the European Commission

Introduction

———— ～ ————

"A bank is a place that will lend you money, if you can prove that you don't need it."

- Bob Hope

Like all of the best turns of phrase, this one has a streak of truth to it. Startups and growing companies are regularly turned away from institutional sources of finance such as banks and venture capitalists. If you have ever tried, maybe some of these sound familiar:

"We require at least 3 years of operating history."

"This doesn't fit our risk criteria."

"It's not scalable enough."

"It's not in our preferred industry."

"You're asking for too much money."

"You're not asking for enough money."

"Come back and see us again in 12 months from now."

The fact is, getting money out of a bank or a venture capital firm is tough. Damn tough. You can spend months going to venture capital pitch meetings, in due diligence, with term sheets flying around, and get nowhere. Or you can go to a bank and have them insist that you put your house on the line as security – and who wants to risk having no roof over their head?

But change is here. Startups and growing companies are able to access capital sourced from large numbers of small investors, using the Internet. Welcome to the world of equity crowdfunding.

The ability to set their own offer terms, promote their company to the public, and let the crowd decide if they are worthy of being funded is a game-changer. It means that startups and growing companies can bypass the financial gatekeepers they have had to kowtow to for so long.

This represents a seismic shift in power between startups and professional investors. The (often unattractive) terms that professional investors tend to offer are no longer the only option for companies seeking funding.

For investors too, equity crowdfunding seems to have come along at exactly the right time. The returns from cash in the bank are at historic lows, and investors are hungry for new options beyond stocks and real estate. At the same time, technological disruption continues apace, and the need is greater than ever to finance the companies building the economy of the future.

Some of the companies featured in these pages are truly ground-breaking. There is Glowee, which has developed a way of lighting through the same biological matter found in jellyfishes. There is Monzo, which has built a smartphone-based bank. There is EkoRent, which provides shared and hourly electric vehicles for hire.

By enabling investment into these kinds of companies at the forefront of the entrepreneurial renaissance, a whole new asset class has been opened up to the portfolios of ordinary investors. Funding startups and growing companies is no longer the exclusive domain of professional and high net worth investors.

But you don't need to be creating world-altering inventions to use equity crowdfunding – within these pages, you will also hear from well-run "traditional" business models (with a unique angle) such as Oppo Ice Cream and Haughton Honey.

Given the broad applicability, little wonder that interest in equity crowdfunding is at an all-time high.

But running an equity crowdfunding campaign is a very steep learning curve. Many entrepreneurs start out with no idea what to do. They know they need money, and they have heard tales of others using equity crowdfunding, but oftentimes that's about the extent of their knowledge. If this sounds anything like you, then this book was written for you.

Many don't know the difference between equity crowdfunding and "rewards crowdfunding" (I'll clear that up at the start of Chapter 1). Others feel overwhelmed by the choice of platforms offering to host them (I'll show you how to choose in Chapter

4). Others will have already got their campaign ready to launch, but don't know how to promote it (in Chapter 7, I'll show you how to form your own marketing action plan).

This book is the world's first resource to draw upon the experience of those with skin in the game – the startups and growing companies that have used equity crowdfunding successfully.

You won't find ideas in this book that *might* work in theory – you will only find the actual strategies from 20 real businesses, which have been battle-tested in the field. The German statesman Otto von Bismarck once said, "Only a fool learns from his own mistakes. The wise man learns from the mistakes of others." So, just as importantly, the 20 companies also share things they tried that *didn't* work.

You will also hear what they really think about equity crowdfunding, having been through it. Even though equity crowdfunding has important advantages over traditional financing methods, it is far from easy.

This book is truly global in scope, and you will also hear from the leading platforms at the forefront of the equity crowdfunding revolution. Those profiled within these pages are from places as diverse as the United States, Canada, the United Kingdom, France, Germany, Sweden, Finland, the Netherlands, Estonia, the Middle East, Australia, and New Zealand.

Finally, the book also contains my own experiences and observations of the industry. A little background on me: my career began in investment banking. I have helped clients in a wide range of industries including media, medical devices, insurance, clean-tech, cosmetics, software, and agriculture.

In my quest to seek out the very best information for this book, I have also traveled extensively: London, Paris, Amsterdam, Sydney, Auckland, and Toronto have all been stops on my tour of global equity crowdfunding over the last 12 months. I might very well be Airbnb's best customer! This book has been the culmination of that effort, and I'm confident you're about to read the very best strategies for equity crowdfunding available today. There is more on my background in the "About The Author" section of the book.

My mission for this book is to help readers to:
- Understand the equity crowdfunding phenomenon.
- Decide whether equity crowdfunding is the best option.
- Choose the best crowdfunding platform.
- Craft their pitch.
- Develop their marketing plan.
- Execute on this plan during the days their offer is live.
- Know what to do next, after the end of the campaign.

Towards that end, I have created a number of downloadable resources and templates that will help you launch your own campaign. Readers can download these for free by visiting **www.nathanrose.me/equity**

The rest of this book is split into nine chapters.

- **Chapter 1** introduces equity crowdfunding with no prior knowledge assumed. We'll go through exactly what happens during a campaign, and which companies are best suited to use it. This section also contains commentary on investor motivations, so you can understand it from the perspective of your would-be investors.

- **Chapter 2** will help you decide whether equity crowdfunding is right for you. I will show you how to compare equity crowdfunding with a range of other funding options — in particular, with rewards crowdfunding, and with traditional angel and venture capital funding. You'll also hear about the fees and expenses to expect.

- **Chapter 3** dives into the wide range of options you will be faced with: non-voting shares vs. voting shares, marketing to accredited vs. non-accredited investors, direct shareholding vs. nominee shareholding — terms which may not mean a lot to you yet, but after this chapter you will have a much better understanding.

- **Chapter 4** explains how to choose from the bewildering array of crowdfunding platforms. Although the different platforms may look similar at first glance, there are crucial differences which matter for your chances of being funded.

- **Chapter 5** gets into framing your pitch, so you can beat the odds and be one of the chosen few to have your offer "go live" on the crowdfunding platform of your choice. I'll show you how to value your company, even if your business is early-stage. You will also learn how to present your pitch in the most compelling way possible.

- **Chapter 6** moves on to the preparation for the campaign. I have included an indicative timeline for a typical offer so you can begin your planning. Next, there is guidance for writing your public business plan, getting things legally signed off, and putting together an amazing video.

- **Chapter 7** explores marketing tactics. This is where the 20 successful crowdfunders tell you exactly what they did to attract interest to their campaigns, so that you can too.

- **Chapter 8** shows how to maintain the momentum after your offer has gone live, through the hustling that needs to carry on throughout the days the campaign is visible to the public. There are also ideas on what to do if things are going more slowly than you had hoped.

- **Chapter 9** covers what to do after the campaign, whether you have failed or succeeded. If you have failed, you need to know what's next. If you have succeeded, you now have to deliver on expectations, communicate with your new shareholders, and start thinking about your next funding round... but not before taking a moment to celebrate!

A Brief Note On Currencies

I have written this book for an international audience. I have used US dollars in cases where a general point needs to be made, because if there is one currency most people everywhere are familiar with, the US dollar is it.

However, for specific case studies where a particular company is involved, I have stayed faithful to the original currency. Exchange rates fluctuate constantly, so converting everything into US dollars would become out of date the moment the book was released. Readers who want to perform the conversion for themselves can easily do so by going online.

Let's Get Started!

I hope you find this book to be a useful resource on your fundraising journey. Tell me what you think of the strategies it contains! Send me an email on **contact@nathanrose.me**. I am especially keen to hear from you if you run a campaign of your own. Let me know about the results you achieved!

Nathan Rose

Chapter 1

The Basics

"Crowdfunding is a way of raising finance by asking a large number of people each for a small amount of money. Until recently, financing a business, project or venture involved asking a few people for large sums of money. Crowdfunding switches this idea around, using the Internet to talk to thousands – if not millions – of potential funders."

- UK Crowdfunding Association

What Is Equity Crowdfunding?

Right from the start, it is important to clear up the difference between "equity crowdfunding" and "rewards crowdfunding," as this is the single biggest point of confusion among those who are new to it. When most people hear "crowdfunding," they automatically think of the type offered by sites like Kickstarter and Indiegogo, without realizing that "crowdfunding" is a much broader term, of which the Kickstarter and Indiegogo variety is but one type.

One reason for this confusion is that businesses can attract money through either form. The fundamental difference is:

- Backers of rewards crowdfunding campaigns are provided with a gift (such as a product, digital download, or experience) in exchange for their pledge.

- Investors in equity crowdfunding get shares of ownership in the company itself.

There have been well-known rewards crowdfunding campaigns which have raised eye-popping sums – for example, the Oculus Rift virtual reality headset garnered US$2.4 million from early backers in 2012 through Kickstarter[1]. The backers of Oculus Rift helped the company get its start and, yes, the backers were duly delivered the virtual reality headset they were promised. But when the company was sold to Facebook in 2014, these backers were only customers, not shareholders. Had Oculus Rift instead been funded through equity crowdfunding,

---

[1] https://www.kickstarter.com/projects/1523379957/oculus-rift-step-into-the-game/description

the ones who contributed the money would have shared in a US$2 billion windfall[2]. That's billion – with a "b". Therein lies the difference: if an investor puts money into an equity crowdfunded company, and the company does well, then they stand to profit. The implications of this distinction are profound.

There is also a difference between equity crowdfunding and the stock market. On the face of it, again the two can seem similar – both are offers of shares in a company to the general public. However, equity crowdfunding is handled through an online platform, without the need for brokers or the stock exchange. Another difference is that raising money through the stock market requires doing an "initial public offering," which means preparing a prospectus, which is a very long and prescribed document, requiring lots of input from expensive lawyers and investment bankers. Equity crowdfunding is therefore simpler and less expensive than an initial public offering, and within reach of companies at an earlier stage.

So, equity crowdfunding generally has four aspects to it[3]:

1. Offers via an online platform.

2. To the general public.

3. For the equity of startups and growing companies.

4. With reduced disclosure obligations, compared to listing on the stock market.

---

[2] http://arstechnica.com/gaming/2014/03/facebook-purchases-vr-headset-maker-oculus-for-2-billion/
[3] It is true that people have started using "equity crowdfunding" in a broader fashion than I have defined here. But this is still useful as a starting point to conceptualize it.

How Does It Work?

So, equity crowdfunding sees investors end up as shareholders in a business, using the Internet. But how does that happen?

Here are some key terms, which will be used throughout:

- **Platforms**: Operate the crowdfunding websites and select the companies to put on their site for potential investors to see. Different platforms have different specialties, and it is worth understanding these in detail. You might hear people call platforms by other names, such as "licensed intermediaries," "broker-dealers," or "portals,"… but the same thing is meant.

- **Companies**: Refer to the ones seeking investment, who offer a share of equity in return for money from investors.

- **Investors**: Are the individuals and organizations that contribute money to the companies, in exchange for a share of equity. They discover investments by visiting platforms.

HOW EQUITY CROWDFUNDING WORKS

Platforms "publish" companies which investors can choose whether to invest in

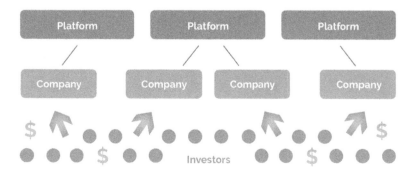

Each campaign needs to set a **target investment amount,** (the minimum amount needed to be raised for the offer to be successfully closed) and a **maximum investment amount** (the maximum amount of money the company will accept).

- If the company set a target of $200,000, but only $150,000 was committed, then the offer would fail and *no* money would change hands – not even the $150,000. Therefore, from the company's perspective it is vital to set the target investment amount at an achievable level.

- If the company set a maximum of $500,000, and investors contributed all of this, then the offer would be "full" and wouldn't be able to accept any more money.

If you have never seen an equity crowdfunding platform before, now would be a good time to go online and check one out. The rest of the section will make a lot more sense if you do.

Go to the website of an equity crowdfunding platform. Any of those mentioned in this book will do. Navigate to where you can see companies seeking funding.

📢 Live offers

Balex Marine

Offer live

$110,250   **20 days**

Total raised   Time left

Balex Marine's Automatic Boat Loader (ABL) is a patented world first disruptive marine technology that is now in market in NZ and expanding into offshore markets. The hydraulically powered ABL lets users launch and retrieve their boat without getting their feet wet and is 3 times faster than an electric winch.

G3 Group

Offer live

$247,756   **17 days**

Total raised   Time left

G3 assists businesses, including a growing international customer base, to manage their data, documents and customer communications, deploying new technologies for maximum reliability and efficiency.

Ubco

Coming soon

The Ubco 2x2 is the world's first production Dual Electric Drive Bike. Designed in New Zealand, the Ubco utilises advances in electric motor design and battery technology to deliver a whisper quiet connected utility vehicle that embraces portable energy.

Initial sales are being driven by a network of dealers established in New Zealand and Australia with growth to come from distributors in the UK, EU and the US. $1.8m has already been raised in this round from new and existing investors.

SIGN UP FOR EARLY ACCESS

You'll receive an email notification and early access to the offer before it's released to the wider public.

27

You will be presented with a list of companies and their investment pitches. Find one that sparks your interest.

Now that you are on an individual campaign page, you will be given some basic information about the company seeking money. In this example, you can see that Balex Marine is the company raising funds. They are seeking a minimum of NZ$296,906 in exchange for 5.21% of their equity. So far they have raised NZ$110,250, which is 37% of the way to their target, and they have 20 days to go. Don't worry if some of these terms don't make sense yet — all will be explained later in the book.

Overview

Balex aims for its Automatic Boat Loader (ABL) to become the new benchmark for the launch and retrieval of trailer-boats. Balex aspires for this remotely controlled system to become what garage door openers are to garages, and dishwashers are to kitchens - once thought an unnecessary luxury, but now the standard.

The ABL is a truly disruptive technology, first to market with no direct competition. This product is specified for alloy and fibreglass hulled boats in the 5-9m range up to 2500kg.

Balex's ABL presents a clear point of difference and value proposition to marine dealers, boat and trailer original equipment manufacturers (OEM) and end consumers in the marine industry. Over time with scale and cost-out the technology has the potential to move from high-end to mainstream consumer pricing brackets.

Scrolling down, you will be able to see additional information. Platforms differ, but you will likely be able to view a short video that introduces the company. There will also be more in-depth written information on the company, including details on the management, strategy, and the financials. There is a place where potential investors can ask questions and receive answers from the company raising funds, which are then displayed for everyone else to see.

If you have ever seen a rewards crowdfunding platform like Kickstarter or Indiegogo, you will have already noticed a lot of similarities, which might go further to explaining why there is so much confusion between rewards crowdfunding and equity crowdfunding. In both incarnations, there's a video, an explanation of the project, and an indication of how much money is being sought.

The differences are subtler. For one thing, equity crowdfunding campaigns need to come up with a valuation. For another, there needs to be a great deal more in-depth information about the whole business model, whereas rewards crowdfunding focuses more singularly on the product – not how much money will be made from it.

Rupert M. Hart, author of *CrowdFund Your StartUp!* colorfully described equity crowdfunding as the "lovechild" result of the "sex" between rewards crowdfunding and traditional startup financing. Well, if it helps you remember the difference between the two, I'm not going to argue!

Which Companies Can Use It?

The best-known use of equity crowdfunding is for startups and growing companies raising funds for growth, giving up a minority stake of ownership, typically in exchange for at least US$50,000 (or the equivalent amount in other currencies), and up to maximum amounts which are legally capped depending on the country in which the raise takes place.

Raising money for growth sees new shares issued. The money raised is deposited into the bank account of the company, in order to finance that growth.

Some founders will want to know if they can use equity crowdfunding to sell some of their existing shares and cash out. While this is possible in theory, it is practically unheard of. "If you want to use the crowd's money to put into your pocket instead of into the business, then the story is not as nice to tell. Money for growth is much more optimistic and has more of a long-term vision behind it. Selling shares comes with a higher level of scrutiny, and it's going to naturally get less interest from the public," says Yannig Roth from WiSEED. Investors in early stage businesses want the founders to be fully invested in the project – not taking money off the table – at least, not until the company is at a later stage.

Although equity crowdfunding is a new phenomenon, it isn't just for young people working in hot startups. Far from it. In fact, many of the companies who I spoke to were being run by people aged in their 40's, 50's, and 60's.

Many diverse business models have used equity crowdfunding, ranging from energy generation, to on-demand food delivery, to education mobile applications. You will hear from representatives from each of these companies, and many more.

Throughout the book, I will group those who tend to have success with equity crowdfunding into two broad categories: **potential big winners**, and **local businesses with a crowd**. I do this because, at times, the most effective tactics diverge depending on which camp a company falls into.

A company which achieves a valuation of at least US$1 billion is known as a 'unicorn' in startup lingo. To have a chance of making it to this magical figure, they need to have great scalability potential, disrupting existing markets or creating an entirely new one. Software, fintech, biotechnology, and medical devices are the sorts of industries that tend to breed potential unicorns. I have avoided the word 'unicorn' in this book, because I don't mean to limit the definition to only companies that can reach a US$1 billion valuation. So instead I use 'potential big winner' – the concept is the same; they are high risk, capital-hungry, innovative young companies looking at fast growth, with a chance of a lucrative exit if they are successful. Such companies can do well with equity crowdfunding because investors can become attracted by the financial returns they might be able to achieve.

'Local businesses with a crowd' are entirely different. They have a large number of passionate users and a strong existing following for their brand. Think food and beverage, cosmetics, and clothing. These businesses may not have the explosive growth prospects of the potential big winners, and therefore don't tend to attract the attention of venture capitalists who are only interested in highly scalable businesses. But, they can be good, worthy businesses nonetheless. They can do well with equity crowdfunding because they can send the details of their offer to lots of people who are already fans of theirs and want to join them on their journey, even if these investors don't expect the prospect of a big payday. There can be other incentives at play, such as a discount on their products and services, or just the feeling of helping out a brand that they already love.

The reason equity crowdfunding has become synonymous with funding startups and growing companies is because this is where the greatest need exists. Andrew J. Sherman, author of *Raising Capital*, has spoken about the 'funding gap' for companies seeking between US$200,000 and US$2 million[4].

Companies seeking capital within this range have a hard time getting funds from their personal savings or friends and family, because they don't have that much money to risk. They also find it difficult to get funding from professional investors with deeper pockets — they are often seen as too risky for banks, and US$2 million is too small for many venture capital funds who are increasingly more interested in investing larger amounts into fewer later-stage companies.

The need to fill this funding gap is extremely pressing, not just for the companies that need the funding, but for the broader economy. In the United States, young companies account for nearly all net new job creation, and American companies under

---

[4] *New Venture Finance.* Coursera class, accessed July 2015.

one-year-old have created an average of 1.5 million jobs per year over the last 30 years[5]. Meanwhile, larger corporations are adding fewer and fewer jobs due to automation, and the jobs they do create are being increasingly offshored to low-wage economies in places such as Asia and Eastern Europe.

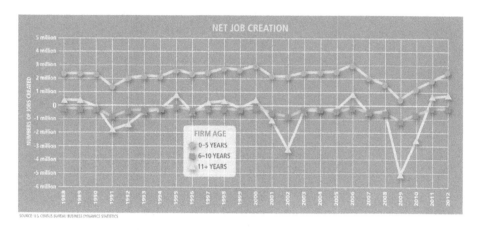

The banks and venture capital firms might be doing the right thing for themselves and their own interest, but they have a role to play as allocators of capital to deserving growing companies (even if they are individually risky). If the banks and venture capital firms are not willing to accept that role, then we need to find a new solution – innovation and job growth depends on it. If we only fund companies whose business models are already proven, or which can offer land and buildings as collateral, then we will be in deep trouble as a society.

In a 2013 report on the potential of crowdfunding, the World Bank opined that equity crowdfunding could be the answer: "Businesses with high growth potential, especially those that

[5] http://www.kauffman.org/what-we-do/resources/entrepreneurship-policy-digest/the-importance-of-young-firms-for-economic-growth

draw on entrepreneurial incubator or accelerator ecosystems, may be especially well-positioned to benefit from crowdfunding investing. Such types of businesses find general market understanding and acceptance, and can leverage the expertise, facilities, mentoring, and peer learning capabilities provided by those ecosystems. *The firms can also gain access to broader markets for fundraising and sales."*[6]

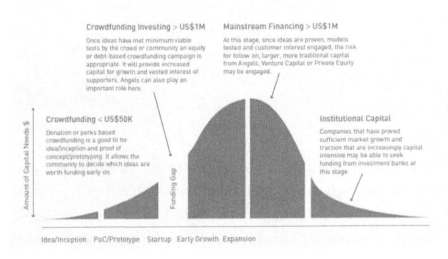

Where Crowdfunding Fits on the Funding Lifecycle

Crowdfunding Investing > US$1M

Once ideas have met minimum viable tests by the crowd or community an equity or debt-based crowdfunding campaign is appropriate. It will provide increased capital for growth and vested interest of supporters. Angels can also play an important role here.

Mainstream Financing > US$1M

At this stage, once ideas are proven, models tested and customer interest engaged, the risk for follow on, larger, more traditional capital from Angels, Venture Capital or Private Equity may be engaged.

Crowdfunding < US$50K

Donation or perks based crowdfunding is a good fit for idea/inception and proof of concept/prototyping. It allows the community to decide which ideas are worth funding early on.

Institutional Capital

Companies that have proved sufficient market growth and traction that are increasingly capital intensive may be able to seek funding from investment banks at this stage.

Amount of Capital Needs $

Funding Gap

Idea/Inception   PoC/Prototype   Startup   Early Growth   Expansion

That last sentence from the World Bank is the really interesting one. It points to the fact that startups and growing companies can use equity crowdfunding to raise money *and* promote their business… *at the same time.*

Since raising money and getting more attention for their business tend to be number one and number two on the list of most critical things a capital-hungry young company needs to do, it is little wonder equity crowdfunding has fired the

---

[6] *Crowdfunding's Potential for the Developing World*, World Bank, 2013

imagination of entrepreneurs to such an extent. "Crowdfunding is as much about user engagement and customer loyalty as it is about the money. There is something to be said about getting more people along for your journey as an entrepreneur," says Ken Nguyen of Republic.

A successful campaign can lead to more interest from media, commercial partners, and consumers. Some companies have reported significant increases in revenue due to exposure from their offers bringing on board loyal shareholder advocates.

Guusto is a great case study for these advantages. "The big benefit to us of doing an equity crowdfunding round was bringing on a number of new brand champions. People who are not only customers, but also promote us to their networks. It helped pour fuel on the fire once our best customers were engaged as shareholders. We were able to better tap into their networks and bring on new customers through them. It's been a great referral channel," says founder Skai Dalziel.

You can download an audio recording of my entire interview with Skai Dalziel at **www.nathanrose.me/equity**

Even though funding startups and growing companies is what equity crowdfunding is best-known for, it is not limited to this. Companies at later stages of development can still use an equity crowdfunding offer to increase their shareholder spread, to substantially improve their business plan, governance, and constitution through the rigor the offer process brings, or to set a valuation anchor for future fundraising rounds. For example, in 2015, Equitise partially crowdfunded the initial public offering of Chinese agricultural giant Dongfang Modern. At the time, Dongfang had annual revenue of AU$133 million — hardly a startup.[7] Offers like this point to the possibilities of equity crowdfunding: new options for a whole new audience of investors who prefer yield, diversification, more-established businesses, or immediate liquidity — rather than venture-capital-like long-term, riskier investments.

What Is New?

Actually, raising money from a large group of investors is nothing particularly new. On crowdfunding news site Crowdfund Insider, Robert Sonsow observed that people have pooled and transferred resources for investment for as long as history can be recounted.[8]

The Statue of Liberty was partly funded by thousands of people throwing coins into donation buckets. Gold mining prospects were often financed by offers of stock. Vast networks of railroads during the industrial revolution were built with the proceeds from bonds offered to the public.

As mentioned earlier, in many respects, an equity crowdfunding campaign is actually similar to an initial public offering (and, as we saw in the case of Dongfang Modern, equity crowdfunding can even happen at the same time as one!).

---

[7] https://equitise.com/project/dongfang-modern-asx-ipo
[8] http://www.crowdfundinsider.com/2016/04/84434-crowdfunding-is-crowdfunding-to-a-crowd-but-any-other-name-would-work-as-well/

Both equity crowdfunding and initial public offerings are offers of shares, which can be subscribed for by the public, with the hope of profiting through dividends or selling the shares in the future for a gain.

So then, what's new about equity crowdfunding? There are two critical aspects of innovation.

1. Technological Advancements

In the past, subscriptions for investments would need to be signed, physically posted, and stamped by a human, but the kind of investing that equity crowdfunding is facilitating is really only possible due to the efficiencies afforded by the Internet. The amount of money involved in equity crowdfunding, with very large numbers of small investors, is too small for the costs associated with the old way of using brokers to subscribe for investments.

Before equity crowdfunding could be possible, we needed the Internet. And we needed to wait for the Internet to become advanced enough to host key information about a company, such as video, images, and so on. The Internet also had to be able to handle electronic signing of documents, accept electronic payments, and for people to get comfortable with it all. None of this would have been possible in, say, 1995.

But the Internet has been good enough to facilitate equity crowdfunding since around the mid-2000's. The real thing holding equity crowdfunding back was the law.

2.   Legal Changes

Legal barriers explain why rewards crowdfunding preceded equity crowdfunding by several years, even though the technology requirements are virtually identical.

Because offering shares in a company is an offer for investment, equity crowdfunding falls under the authority of securities regulators – the likes of the Securities and Exchange Commission (SEC) in the United States, and the Financial Conduct Authority (FCA) in the United Kingdom. Anytime securities regulators are involved, there are great deal many more rules and restrictions on what can and can't be done. Therefore, the law had to change on a country-by-country basis for it to be legal for startups and growing companies to market shares to the general public through equity crowdfunding.

Basically[9], before changes in the law enabled equity crowdfunding, the only way to offer shares to the public was to put together a **prospectus** – a very long and legalistic document, which is prohibitively expensive for a young, growing company to prepare. Without a prospectus, shares could still be marketed to sophisticated and high net worth investors, and close family, friends, and business associates, but this is a much smaller audience and shuts the general public out.

Due to red tape and cost - young, growing companies were prevented from seeking investment from the general public, and the general public were shut out from this type of investing.

---

[9] These are sweeping generalizations of complex securities laws across many different countries. I am glossing over a lot of detail, but this summary is fine for our purposes.

More recently, regulators have relaxed their position. Equity crowdfunding has come to life because most developed countries have created special exemptions to the securities laws to enable small amounts of capital to be raised from the public, with a lower burden of disclosure.

So in the countries where equity crowdfunding has become legal, almost anyone can now invest in startups and growing companies, so long as they are of legal age, have an Internet connection, and have a bank account with some money in it — a big change from just a few years ago.

What Are The Rules?

This book is focusing on campaign strategies which are globally applicable. Securities regulations are generally established on a country-by-country basis and with nearly 200 countries in the world, it would be a book in itself to explain the status of equity crowdfunding regulation in every single one of them. Even so, I have decided to provide an overview of the relevant regulations in the English-speaking countries of the OECD.

A reminder of the book's disclaimer is necessary at this point – this is for general information purposes only, it is not legal advice, and the information may have changed since this edition of the book was published. Check with relevant legal counsel before taking any action.

This analysis focuses on options available to issuers under reduced disclosure obligations (vs. a prospectus), which are allowed to be marketed to ordinary investors – as in, those who do not pass any kind of sophisticated or high net worth threshold. Some countries have moved faster than others, and different countries have taken different approaches to regulation, ranging from very liberal to very protectionist.

It is impossible to cleanly provide all the detailed information on the many exemptions in all of the countries in a table like this. I am showing the regulations most in keeping with what I consider the "spirit" of equity crowdfunding. Because this book is for an international audience, I will not go into all the different exemptions in depth, but you should know that there may be more possibilities than are shown here.

Equity crowdfunding regulations frequently change. The most up-to-date version of this table can be downloaded at **www.nathanrose.me/equity**

	UK	USA	Canada	New Zealand	Australia
Raise limit / 12 mo	€8 million	US$1 million	CA$1.5 million	NZ$2 million	AU$5 million
Ordinary investors allowed?	Yes	Yes	Yes	Yes	Yes
Investment limit per investor (ordinary)	Under 10% of net assets in total	$2,000 per offer OR 5% income per offer if income is <$100k	$2,500 per offer (+ Some provinces have extra limits for crowdfunding in total)	None	$10,000 per offer
Investment limit per investor (accredited)	None	$100k OR 10% lesser income / net worth >100k	$25k per offer (+ Some provinces have extra limits for crowdfunding in total)	None	None
Regulator	Financial Conduct Authority	Securities and Exchange Commission	Province-by-Province Regulation	Financial Markets Authority	Australian Securities and Investments Commission
Other	Very attractive tax relief (SEIS / EIS)	Explicit "no exemption" of platform and intermediary liability	Many different levels of crowdfunding exemptions	Not specifically limited to small enterprises	Restricted to "public" and "proprietary limited private companies"

To repeat, these rules only apply to offers to ordinary investors and without a prospectus. More recently, the equity crowdfunding platforms have extended their services to include offers solely to sophisticated and accredited investors, parallel offers in multiple countries, and prospectus offers. See Chapter 3 for more detail on these extensions of equity crowdfunding beyond its traditional meaning.

Investor Motivations

It is vital to understand the motivations of would-be investors.

It may sound obvious, but many founders forget that people who commit money through equity crowdfunding are *investing*, which is not the same as *buying* your product or service. This means the messaging needs to be quite different. Most owners are much more familiar with marketing their product or service to customers than marketing their whole business model to investors. Keep in mind: there is every chance of securing money from people who have no interest in using your product or service, so you must instead sell them on your company's ability (or potential) to generate revenue and ultimately, profit.

Investor motivations can be separated according to the two categories we introduced earlier: the 'potential big winners' and the 'local businesses with a crowd'.

Potential Big Winners

Crowdfunded potential big winners allow ordinary investors to gain exposure to venture-capital-like investments in their portfolio. Previously, these companies had to rely on professional investors for funding. High minimum investment sizes, typically of at least US$20,000 per company, made early-stage investing an exclusive domain. Ordinary investors didn't have the cash to play in the space without putting an unreasonable proportion of their net worth at risk, even if the law had allowed them to do so (which it did not).

Now that equity crowdfunding is here, much lower minimum investment sizes mean it is a realistic option for people with ordinary, middle-class levels of net worth to buy into several crowdfunding offers without risking their entire life savings.

Here is how it could work: an investor invests in twenty equity crowdfunded companies at $1,000 each – an outlay of $20,000 (which is not an unreasonably large sum in the context of the amount we invest in property and retirement portfolios across a lifetime). Sixteen of these twenty companies completely fail, two are moderately successful and double in value, and two are large successes and increase in value by twenty times. This would see the portfolio rise in value to $44,000, which is a return of more than twice the initial outlay of $20,000, despite a failure rate of 80%.

This is the sort of outcome venture capitalists hope for – they invest in many opportunities, expecting most will fail, but that the successes will be large enough to more than offset the failures. The proportion of right and wrong does not matter — what counts is the accumulated payoff.

Of course, this only works when an investor has access to a sufficiently high-quality pool of companies. If all of them fail, or the wins are not large enough, the math will not add up to be positive. It is also possible all twenty could fail. That's a risk, which is why it is important to limit the exposure to early-stage companies to a small proportion of a total portfolio.

Local Businesses With A Crowd

The investor motivations for local businesses with a crowd are more about already-loyal customers deepening their relationship with a brand and potentially getting discounts on products they already consume. "Professional investors tend to look at companies on a purely financial return perspective. Crowd investors are looking at the financial returns too, but are also looking at it from an emotional, and goodwill standpoint. They love the product, they love the idea, they think the team is great, or there is some existing relationship already," says Sean Burke of FrontFundr.

Given the different motivations at play, equity crowdfunding for local businesses with a crowd can at times seem more similar to rewards crowdfunding campaigns. If the investors are putting their money in for non-financial reasons, then they might have a share of equity, but the real motivation isn't to maximize their return.

Crowdfunding for local businesses is part of a broader trend of people using their money to change the world for the better.

The rise of socially responsible investment funds is another indicator that people want to do good with their savings.

In the book *Equity Crowdfunding: Transforming Customers Into Loyal Owners,* Jonathan Frutkin observes that equity crowdfunding can effectively turn a local business into a mutual society, changing the relationship between customer and company. When customers also have a stake in the company's success, they will use the products and services of that company more often, tell their friends about the company, and be more engaged than if they were only a normal customer.

What better way to grow than leveraging a crowd of passionate advocates by giving them a real stake in your success? If you were a shareholder of your local café through equity crowdfunding, and you had to choose between the one you were a part-owner of, and the one next door for your morning caffeine hit, which would you choose? Which one will you encourage your friends to go to? Which one will you be willing to support when they ask you to like and share their social media, turn up to their special events, and provide feedback on new products?

Established local businesses are an entirely different risk proposition from potential big winners – they are generally lower-risk, but are also far less likely to be headed for the big exit. Investors don't stand to win big by investing in local businesses in the same way they can with the potential big winners — but then, they don't expect to. For investors in local business, it is more about supporting a company that they like.

Does The Crowd Know What They Are Investing In?

A common criticism of equity crowdfunding is that investors don't properly understand the risks they are taking. Critics also claim the rules that used to be in place which restricted investment in startups by ordinary investors were there for good reason, and that they have been somewhat carelessly tossed out.

These points need to be addressed. As a company raising funds, it is important to understand all the issues and perceptions that surround equity crowdfunding.

Are startups too risky for ordinary investors to be allowed access to? Your view will depend on the degree to which you believe the government needs to 'protect people from themselves for their own good'.

I will say this: We barely regulate people's ability to walk into a betting shop with their life savings and place it all on the outcome of a horse race. It seems a little silly to make startups, which are creating real jobs and selling real products and services, more restricted to invest in than outright gambling, where your return will be based on the speed of a four-legged animal with a small person riding on their back, wearing colorful silks and white jodhpurs.

A balance needs to be struck between protecting people and giving them the right, as adults, to do what they want to do with their own money. We need to protect people from deceptive or misleading statements, but a blanket ban on all startup investing is surely overkill.

Besides, there are plenty of risk disclosures on the platforms and within the pitch documents that make plain to anyone reading that equity crowdfunding carries significant risks. To take an excerpt from the risk disclosure from one platform:

> *"Most startups fail, and it is significantly more likely that you will lose all of your invested capital than that you will see a return of capital or a profit. You should not invest more money through the platform than you can afford to lose without altering your standard of living.*
>
> *The value of investments and the income from them can fluctuate and may fall and there is no certainty that an investor will get back any part of his investment. Any investment... should be viewed as a long-term and illiquid investment.*
>
> *Startups rarely pay dividends. This means that... even if it is successful you are unlikely to see any return of capital or profit until you are able to sell your shares in the investee company. Even for a successful business, this is unlikely to occur for a number of years from the time you make your investment."*

It really doesn't get much clearer than that.

But there's much more to investor education than simply stating the risks. The best equity crowdfunding platforms take their responsibility to educate investors very seriously. They produce articles, podcasts, and videos about early-stage company investing, and they hold seminars and workshops which anybody can attend to learn more. The platforms are taking a long-term view of the space, and they are a leading force for increasing society's financial savvy.

To become licensed, equity crowdfunding platforms in most countries need to go through a formal process with the relevant regulators. Then, once operational, the long-term business model of a platform is highly aligned with developing a reputation for having high-quality investment opportunities, and cultivating a large, engaged investor audience. So there are self-regulating forces within the industry that should ensure the startups being listed are worthy of it.

You now have a handle on equity crowdfunding and how it works. Companies can use it to raise money from the general public, through the Internet. This new medium has an important part to play in closing the funding gap, for companies too large for friends and family, yet too small for banks and venture capital. Equity crowdfunding is suitable for many different types of businesses, which can be broadly grouped together as either local businesses with a crowd or potential big winners. The investor motivations are different in each case – investors in local businesses with a crowd can gain a sense of connectedness and deepen their loyalty, whereas investors in potential big winners have the opportunity to make a lot of money, if the risk pays off.

With the basics handled, next we turn to the question of: is equity crowdfunding the best option, given your circumstances?

Chapter 2

---〜---

Is Equity Crowdfunding Right For You?

"If there's one thing that people considering equity crowdfunding need to know, it is that it takes significantly longer than you expect. You need to be prepared for that."

– Nathan Lawrence (Raised NZ$816,000 on Snowball Effect)

Sorry to say this, but just putting up a campaign page will not result in the Internet showering you with cash.

Ken Nguyen of Republic puts it very well: "Some founders come to us and think, 'oh, geez, if we go up on the platform, then the money will just roll in.' No! That's not how marketing works, and that's not how fundraising works. If you're going to do equity crowdfunding, you've got to hustle, you've got to knock on every door. It's a lot of work!"

Many of the founders I spoke to emphasized how much work equity crowdfunding turned out to be. When you look at a successful campaign, all you see is the page with a few words describing the business, a video which is a few minutes long at the most, and the money just seems to pour in. It looks so easy! But although it may not look like much, everything that has gone onto that campaign page will have been gone over, rewritten, and verified countless times. The money coming in is the result of extensive planning and outreach efforts.

Startups and growing companies are always stretched for resources, and adding a capital raising into the mix can stretch some companies to their breaking point. Various campaigns surveyed in the course of putting this book together said the founder needed to devote anywhere from 20 hours a week, to over 40 hours a week, for anywhere between two and six months. Yes, you read that correctly — running an equity crowdfunding campaign can be a full-time job.

Rethinking Your Need For Capital

The best way to raise money is (and always will be) to sell things to customers. That way, you retain control of the company *and* grow the value of it.

Ultimately, all forms of outside financing are relying on your ability to sell things to customers at some point. Debt investors are backing your ability to sell things to customers so you can pay them back with interest. Equity investors are backing your ability to build a system of selling things to customers so that their stake becomes more valuable. Offering debt and equity are borrowing against your future ability to sell things to customers.

Many founders have been sold on the idea of raising capital and presenting themselves in a way that will be attractive to investors, without considering the reverse: *whether having investors is attractive to them, as founders!* Maybe you have been seduced by the stories of the heroes of Silicon Valley who have built billion-dollar empires on the back of getting funded, and assume that this is the one true path to success and glory.

Business models are easier than ever to test and implement with minimal funding. Websites can be built, minimum viable products designed, and marketing done – all using techniques which are cheap or free. Do you really need to raise money, or do you just need to hustle harder using your existing resources?

The Purpose Of A Business

Some people assume that the purpose for a business to exist is to *generate profits* for shareholders. But this is not the full story. The real purpose of a business is to *serve the interests* of the shareholders. Profit is one interest, but not the only one – especially for founders who spend a lot of their time in the business. Their interests are served by a combination of profit *and* enjoyment.

If self-reliance and total control are the main things that draw you to being an entrepreneur, then efforts to raise equity could result in removing the very things you enjoy most about working for yourself. With shareholders, you must consider the interests of other people in your decision-making. For those who value independence above all, this loss of autonomy is unlikely to be worth the money.

Investors will be pushing your business to move in a direction that maximizes their return on the capital they have invested. That direction might not be the same thing as what maximizes the founder's enjoyment.

It's your business and you get to run it however you want... until you have shareholders who force you to take into account what *they* want too. Some founders simply do not have growth at the core of why they are operating. It could be more important to them that they are doing interesting work, or perhaps they don't care to grow the company beyond the level that supports their lifestyle.

Investors who expect growth and profit will not be happy if the founder they have invested in wants to take that random month off to lie on a beach because they feel like it, or refuses to expand just because they prefer to work less.

In addition, investors are often looking for a way to eventually make a profit on their stake through a sale (more on that in Chapter 9). Maybe you can't imagine ever selling your business. Maybe you enjoy the work, and you enjoy the learning and personal growth that comes with running it.

At the core of these problems is the misalignment between what the founders want and what the investors want. Some entrepreneurs gain satisfaction from *growing* a business, whereas others gain more satisfaction from *having* a business. Which are you?

A final point: if your business relies on your unique skills, it is less suitable to raise equity. I once had a chess coach who gave me one-on-one lessons. He had many students learning from him and he made quite a nice living, but it wasn't the sort of business he could ever sell. He was a top player – one of the best in the country, and due to his skill borne of years of practice, his client base could only ever reasonably be served by him. All investible companies have some sort of asset that sets them apart from their competition, and the systems in place to allow continuity in the event the founder ever left. It is only suitable to seek investors if your business has the potential to be an asset that could one day operate without you.

If, after reading the above, you realize that having outside shareholders isn't for you, you can stop reading. You have been saved countless hours of time, not to mention plenty of mental anguish. You have been prevented from chasing something that you never wanted in the first place.

What About The Benefits Of Raising Money?

Thomas Adner, the managing director of Caliente, explains why his business decided to raise funds: "We were running the business part-time, because it was not yet at a stage where we could pay ourselves enough to focus on it full-time. This was extremely difficult. To launch a new brand in the beverage market we needed to do a significant push. We needed to go all-in. Continuing to work on it on evenings and weekends wouldn't take us anywhere."

You may not have the luxury of growing slowly. If you operate in a fast-moving industry, opportunities can be fleeting — if you don't get there first, someone else will. If you had started an Internet search engine in the early 1990's, you might have had a chance of gaining world preeminence, but if you tried to do it today, there is practically no chance you would be able to compete with Google.

The additional resources provided by outside investors can help you to get to where you are going faster – whether that is through investing in additional marketing effort, opening in new locations, or by developing new products.

If you want growth, then having investors is a great way to hold your feet to the fire. Investors want to see growth, so having investors will force your business toward a more growth-oriented path. Investors are like having a personal trainer constantly checking up on your progress and giving you a whip if you are slacking off. This added pressure and commercial discipline is not to everyone's liking, but it can get you better growth results than self-motivation can.

Fundraising Alternatives

With that out of the way, we will assume from now on that yours really is a business that should raise capital, and that you are a founder who wants to make that happen.

There are many different ways of funding a company. It is worthwhile to evaluate equity crowdfunding against the many alternatives. After reading this list, you may discover that other ways of financing could be a better fit.

1.   Personal Savings

Bootstrapping with personal funds is something that just about all company founders have needed to do at some stage.

One of the first questions that outside investors will ask is: 'How much have you personally invested yourself?' If you can't show you are taking a significant monetary risk, outside investors will probably be leery about giving you any of their money for you to play with. If you are very young and have not had the time to build up substantial financial resources that you could use, then they might be more understanding. The point is, investors want to see that you are personally invested in the venture before they will be willing to join you.

Using personal savings has the advantage of allowing you to keep full control. But if your personal resources are not large, your frugality may be a hindrance to your venture's potential and slow down your growth. Using personal resources is also riskier for you, because it is your money at stake, but this also means you will be more careful with it. Learning how to do more with less is a valuable discipline which will serve you well, even once your venture has grown far beyond the bootstrapping stage.

2.   Family And Friends

One step beyond your own personal resources are the resources of those within your immediate circle. They know you, they can see your passion, and they may back your idea on more favorable terms than those further removed from you.

Just because you have a close relationship with family and friends doesn't mean the agreement can be too informal. Always put terms into writing. Even if your friends and family don't insist on it, you should. Perhaps your family or friends think of a cash contribution as a gift, more than an investment. If that's the case, that's fine, but make it crystal clear what (if any) shareholding they gain. Don't be scared to get a lawyer involved – it could save a lot of heartache down the line.

Also, consider the worst-case scenario and whether you and they are prepared to go through with that. Losing the capital of financial investors will not be a fun experience, but losing the money of family and friends can be downright miserable if it ruins relationships. Can you handle that prospect? Do your friends and family understand the risks? Think about this very carefully before taking money from those near and dear to you.

3.   Government Grants

In many places, generous government grants are in place to help businesses get their start. These grants are the most underappreciated of all early-stage company financing options.

Some grants are conditional – for example, they could require you to hire a minimum number of local staff. You should definitely take the time to understand the implications of these conditions before signing up to a grant program. But in many cases, government grants are literally free money to foster entrepreneurship and jobs. The government doesn't become a shareholder, and it doesn't expect you to repay the money later.

The reason government grants are so often overlooked is founders find it difficult to navigate all the various programs that are out there; grants can be available from both local and central government, and from many different agencies. To help with your search, identify government information services that can point you in the right direction.

Securing a government grant is also a great credibility indicator if you ever pitch to investors in the future.

4.   Bank Loans

Borrowing money to grow your company costs in interest repayments, but this interest may end up being a lot cheaper than giving up a large piece of equity in your company.

It is rare for companies to get bank financing at the very early stage, because they can't offer enough security for the bank to become comfortable. You may be asked to personally guarantee the loan against other assets you have (such as your house).

Personally guaranteeing a loan means you are effectively doing the same thing as using your personal savings – in both cases, the loss in the event of a business failure is yours to bear. For some entrepreneurs, putting their personal assets on the line is untenable, which is why they seek equity investment instead.

Even if the bank would give your company a loan without your personal guarantee, you may still choose to provide a personal guarantee anyway in exchange for a more favorable interest rate. The less risky it is for the bank, the less you will pay in interest.

5. Co-Founders

Any time a company is founded with more than one person, different founders will bring different things to the table; you can have a programming co-founder, a marketing co-founder, a business-development co-founder... and you can have a financial backer as a co-founder too.

Those who contribute money instead of day-to-day work are known as 'silent partners.' However, the best silent partners in early-stage companies are not silent! The best silent partners will help by determining the strategic direction – often financial backers are older, with experience, taking on a mentorship role. Or maybe they are half-silent, working on the business part-time, but contributing extra capital. The possibilities are only limited to what is acceptable to all parties involved.

As always, make sure expectations are clear, and in writing, regarding how much money and time each of the co-founders are expected to contribute.

6. Incubators / Accelerators

Incubators and accelerators are for promising startups, providing a low-cost or no-cost shared office environment, support services, and sometimes seed capital in exchange for equity.

Depending on the quality of the program, the experience of being in an incubator or accelerator can increase the chance of a startup thriving. Many founders find the environment of being around other startups to be invigorating, and these programs tend to facilitate a lot of learning in a short time.

Incubators and accelerators usually require founders to commit to relocating themselves to the premises for a set period. This can be disruptive to operations and isn't for everyone.

Because incubators and accelerators focus on very early-stage companies, the amount of capital they can offer is usually quite small. Companies needing several hundred thousand dollars or more will need to look elsewhere. However, companies that have been through an incubator or accelerator program can seek larger amounts of funding from contacts they make there; the introductions they can provide can help get a foot in the door with investors who have deeper pockets.

You have already heard that equity crowdfunding can be conceptualized as being a mixture of rewards crowdfunding and venture capital. Since these are perceived to be the alternatives which are closest to equity crowdfunding, the next two sections weigh up the pros and cons of them in more depth.

Rewards Crowdfunding Comparison

The difference between rewards crowdfunding and equity crowdfunding was introduced at the start of Chapter 1. To repeat, rewards crowdfunding and equity crowdfunding campaigns look and feel similar to each other – both have a video, a public Q&A forum, payments done through an online platform, and so on. The difference is: rewards crowdfunding offers people the chance to back you based on the promise of receiving a product or experience, while equity crowdfunding investors get shares in the company in exchange for the cash.

Advantages Of Rewards Crowdfunding

The biggest advantage of rewards crowdfunding is that the founders get to raise money without giving up any shares in their company. They gain customers, not investors, and therefore only need to deliver a product to them rather than have them around forever as shareholders.

There are also fewer barriers to launching a rewards crowdfunding offer, because your company will not be subject to such intensive checks from the platform, and there are fewer regulations involved. This means rewards crowdfunding can raise smaller amounts of money, with fewer upfront expenses.

Because rewards crowdfunding is often based around a product launch, you will get better feedback on the product than in equity crowdfunding. One thing that often happens in rewards crowdfunding is the backers will tell the creator what features they want to see, leading to some very useful customer engagement while in the design phase.

Now let's run through the advantages of equity crowdfunding:

Typically Raises A Lot More Money

While rewards crowdfunding campaigns have raised hundreds of thousands and even millions of dollars, this level of uptake is very uncommon. Anyone can *launch* a rewards crowdfunding campaign, but not just anyone can *close* one with a meaningful amount of money raised. You might be the one to beat the odds, but when it comes to raises in the six figures and up, the success rate with equity crowdfunding is much higher.

Suitable For More Kinds Of Businesses

Rewards crowdfunding can work great for certain products, but what if you are in the business of something that can't be handled and shipped? Or what if what you create is very complex or very expensive? It's difficult to shoehorn, say, a prosthetic limb business into a rewards crowdfunding perk. But equity crowdfunding enables B2B companies, service businesses, and businesses which aren't naturally publicly-facing to raise funds.

Expert Feedback

Running an equity crowdfunding campaign will expose you to a more rigorous process than rewards crowdfunding. You will have outsiders look much more critically at your entire business as an investment proposition before you can launch. You will need to have your shareholder agreement, company constitution, and share structure cleaned up. These processes are a lot of work, but they are highly valuable exercises, especially if you hope to sell the company in the future.

Valuation Proof

One thing that owners really struggle with when selling their business is valuation, and justifying it to the buyers. An equity crowdfunding offer is a great place to kick off negotiations. If your campaign is successful, the public has validated an equity value for your company. A rewards crowdfunding campaign shows something different; mostly your ability to execute on marketing, and that demand for your product exists. Some companies have used equity crowdfunding even when they don't actually need the money, just to prove their valuation prior to an initial public offering or sales process.

Smart Money

Some platforms will ask you to anchor your equity crowdfunding offer with a **lead investor** (as in, someone from an angel investing background, who contributes a large sum towards your goal as a way of validating the proposition). Having that 'smart money' expertise in there can be a valuable source of contacts and advice. Rewards crowdfunding money tends to be silent on other areas of your business development – your rewards crowdfunding backers don't really care if your business is making money or not, so long as they get the reward you promised them.

Marketing Benefits

Journalists are approached daily with requests to feature the latest rewards campaign of the day. Some journalists have even added a filter to their email inboxes to send any email that contains the words 'Kickstarter' or 'Indiegogo' straight to their trash folder! By contrast, equity crowdfunding platforms tend to have just a handful of offers live at a time, rather than hundreds or thousands, making it easier to stand out in a *crowded* media landscape.

More Enduring Relationship

Pre-ordering a reward is one thing — creators and backers will keep in touch while the reward is being delivered. But often, that can be it. When you bring on an equity investor, the relationship is far more binding. It's like the difference between dating and marriage.

Working Together

Rewards crowdfunding can also work well together with equity crowdfunding. EkoRent provides electric vehicles for hire around the city of Helsinki, Finland. In November 2015, they raised €12,000 on rewards crowdfunding platform Joukon Voima. "We got a lot of press from our rewards campaign, and it enabled us to bring EkoRent to a few additional service stations," says CEO Juha Suojanen. A few months later, EkoRent followed this up with a €171,000 successful raise on the equity crowdfunding platform Invesdor. Since EkoRent had done their prior rewards campaign, they had already practiced campaigning, prepared some of the materials, and knew how long things would take. The more practice you get at crowdfunding, the better you will become.

Since rewards crowdfunding is done for new product launches, and equity crowdfunding tends to be for businesses with a bit more traction, it seems logical to do what EkoRent did and do your rewards crowdfunding campaign before equity crowdfunding. But Ampler Bikes turned this on its head when it raised €91,500 through equity crowdfunding on Fundwise in December 2015, and then followed it up with a US$143,000 Indiegogo rewards campaign in May 2016.

Ardo Kaurit of Ampler Bikes explains: "When we did our first fundraising, our product was not yet ready – so we couldn't actually promise people a bike until more money and time had been spent on development. We were also out of budget for a proper marketing campaign. For us, equity crowdfunding allowed us to complete development, provided funds for marketing, and gave us experience with running a crowdfunding process before we launched on Indiegogo. Equity crowdfunding also had the benefit of surrounding us with a group of intelligent people who were interested in our success and were willing to put in the effort."

Financial Investor Comparison

Angel investors, venture capital, and private equity can be grouped together as **financial investors**. Before equity crowdfunding, they were just about the only ones willing to take a risk on early-stage companies.

Those who get a financial investor gain a partner, along with their money. This active role is one reason why some company founders still prefer financial investors instead of equity crowdfunding; they get to deal with a small number of large investors who are highly incentivized to drive the company forward.

"There are times where a startup would be better with angel or VC funding," admits Yannig Roth of WiSEED, "If your business is not the kind that can expect much traction from a public campaign, or if the benefit your company offers is tricky to explain in a crisp manner, it could be a lot of effort better spent on talking to financial investors. If you have a great company being highly sought by venture capital, you could get the money with less effort. But don't forget that crowdfunding offers more than just the money – it offers engagement, visibility and advocacy too".

The marketing effort is much larger in an equity crowdfunding campaign. If you can get the money more quickly from a financial investor, then that saved time can instead be put towards other business efforts.

For a lot of startups, though, the idea of a financial investor is anathema to their company culture. Alicja Chlebna runs Naturalbox, which delivers ethical, organic snacks, health, and beauty products. She says: "No banker would share the passion I have for my business. Most venture capitalists are pretty arrogant, greedy, and difficult to work with, from what I know."

Strong words, but Alicja isn't alone in feeling this way.

Now, let's be clear that not all venture capitalists fit this description. There are a lot of great people in VC that generate win-win environments for themselves and the companies they work with. Nonetheless, it must be said that people in the VC industry are mostly male, and tend to come from similar backgrounds; elite universities, and the corporate world. It should not be surprising that among the melting pot of diversity that entrepreneurs represent, some won't gel with people from this VC culture. These entrepreneurs are not necessarily less worthy of being funded – but until now, if they needed funding, they haven't had much choice but to submit themselves to a culture they don't identify with. Retaining control of culture is a real advantage of equity crowdfunding.

Here are the other factors which must be weighed when choosing between financial investors and equity crowdfunding.

More Open Access

Mark Hughes of Tutora had this to say about their efforts to reach out to venture capital: "They are incredibly hard to access. The main pushback was we were too small. Even though we had real customers and real revenue, they were just looking for something bigger. The other pushback we had was: 'we don't know who you are.' Venture capital in London is very much a closed, old-boys shop. They only want people coming to them who have come with a recommendation. It makes it really hard if you come from somewhere like the north of England where there's just not a lot of venture capital activity going on."

Sandra Rey's attempts to reach out to venture capital were frustrated by the fact that Glowee didn't seem to fit with any of the firms they approached. "We have a very new and disruptive product – Glowee uses biotechnology to generate biological lighting. But when we were going to biotech venture capitalists, we were told that we weren't purely biotech enough. Then, when we went to clean-tech funds, they said they didn't help with companies in the biotech space! Glowee just didn't fit with the parameters they had already decided on."

Better Outcome On Valuation

Whether equity crowdfunding valuations are higher than those negotiated by financial investors is a hot topic, and the startups and platforms I surveyed were divided on the question. But because the power dynamic is more in the company's favor with equity crowdfunding, the balance of evidence suggests that higher valuations are indeed being achieved.

Venture capitalists are highly experienced in making investments. *It's what they do.* When it comes time to talk numbers, they have a massive skill advantage over company founders who may be complete novices, or have been through it a handful of times at most. As the valuation is being negotiated, founders can feel like they are playing against a chess grandmaster, while they barely know how the pieces move.

You may have heard financial investors bemoaning the valuations being achieved in equity crowdfunding as 'unrealistic.' It is hard to know whether to take these complaints seriously, or dismiss them as vested interests protecting their patch – the same way the traditional taxi drivers protest the advent of Uber. "How awful to think the VC's position as the exclusive source of capital is being disrupted. Is it ironic that technology will eat its own creator?" quipped Howard Marks of StartEngine Crowdfunding.[10]

Better Outcome On Investment Terms

One of the most important ways that venture capitalists make money is through the terms they insert into the deal. "The terms from venture capital are always restrictive," says Laurence Cook of Pavegen. "They want board seats, control, liquidation preferences, restrictive terms on the founders – all things which don't favor the company raising money. Venture capital firms make their money by negotiating hard. That's their job, and they are very, very good at it. By raising money through the crowd, we were able to raise the money on our own terms."

The restrictive terms inserted by venture capital serve to protect their downside while still offering many multiples of upside, often at the expense of the company founders. It seems like they want to have it both ways – and indeed, that is exactly what they want. Again, founders can try to negotiate, but their position is weak – they need the money, and they are afraid of the VC walking away.

By contrast, equity crowdfunding sees standardized documents which effectively manage the real need for preemption rights and avoiding dilution, but in a way that is fair for both new investors *and* founders.

---

[10] http://crowdfundbeat.com/2016/04/25/why-vcs-do-not-like-equity-crowdfunding/

Publicity

One of the main reasons to conduct an equity crowdfunding offer is to build awareness of a company among customers. You will hear many examples of how this manifested itself throughout the book. What is often overlooked is how effective it can be for getting introductions to new suppliers, board members, and other partnerships. When you put your company out there in such a public forum, people can notice and be attracted to your company in so many ways. The ability to put your name out there to the world through a public equity crowdfunding campaign can be a game-changer through the exposure it gives. Conversely, a deal with financial investors is done behind closed doors.

Remember though that publicity can be a double-edged sword. It is great if your offer succeeds, because everyone will see that. But equity crowdfunding failures will also be there in the public arena for all to see, while a failed deal with financial investors will never see the light of day beyond the boardroom.

Broad Shareholder Base

An enlarged shareholder base can provide new passionate shareholder advocates.

Venture capitalists are also shareholder advocates through the networks and introductions they provide. But for the sheer number of advocates, equity crowdfunding wins hands down. Imagine having dozens, or even hundreds, of new people who are incentivized to look out for your interests, because your financial interests are now the same as their financial interests!

Another point needs to be addressed here, which is the fear that equity crowdfunding will make a company less attractive to financial investors in the future, due to the large number of shareholders making the share register 'difficult to deal with' for potential future buyers.

"Really, it depends on the firm," says Bret Conkin of Crowdfund Suite, "There's certainly a group of crowdfunding non-believers in the venture capital community, but there is an increasing percentage who are buying into it. In some cases, they are even combing through the crowdfunding platforms as a way of finding new companies to invest in."

There will always be some people who don't like dealing with new ways of doing things, but something like the share register is a very minor thing that can be worked out, if needed. Ultimately, business performance matters more. If your business is going well enough, financial investors will look past a messy register, or find a way to restructure things.

As Skai Dalziel of Guusto points out: "The bigger risk is not having a successful company. The goal is to get an operating business that generates profits. If crowdfunding is a way to get there, great."

In the future, you would much rather have a thriving business, thanks to the funds you raised and the growth you achieved, even if financial investors later show resistance to investing in it because it was funded through equity crowdfunding.

Working Together

When founders think of equity crowdfunding, typically they are envisaging having investors who don't bring anything to the business apart from the money. When weighing this against bringing on a few financial investors that promise to lend their time to the business, founders become sold on the idea of having this 'smart money' on their side.

But when a company runs an equity crowdfunding campaign, large investors *aren't* excluded! In fact, the platforms will *encourage* you to bring financial investors to your offer.

An equity crowdfunding raise of $1 million may consist of one investor putting in $300,000, two contributing $100,000 each, six doing $25,000 each, and the remainder in smaller amounts. That single investor who contributed $300,000 may be the sort of person you could add to your board of directors. The lesson is: equity crowdfunding *can* involve smart money investors, if you choose.

Tom Britton of SyndicateRoom points to the efficiencies that equity crowdfunding platforms can bring, even to the process of getting new large investors to commit. "In the old days, when a round needed to be filled by several angels or VCs, each new investor would try to re-negotiate the valuation, go over the terms again and try to get preferences over the others. It was just a pain. But by bringing that process online, once a company finds their first investor, they put the terms on the platform, and any investors that come afterward must agree to the terms originally set."

Fees

There are usually costs involved with raising capital through equity crowdfunding. How much? I hate to say that *'the answer depends,'* but it really does. The main factors which determine your expenses are: how much marketing outreach you will undertake (and whether you do the work yourself, or outsource it to agencies), as well as the regulations you must comply with.

"It depends on how well-prepared you already are. Having your house in order will mean the transaction costs will be much lower. But if you need lots of help from professionals, then the expenses can mount up," says Will Mahon-Heap of Equitise.

There are two types of costs: **upfront costs** which need to be paid regardless of the campaign outcome, and **contingent costs** which only need to be paid if the offer succeeds.

Founders should be most concerned about upfront costs. Capital-hungry companies hoping to raise money usually can't afford to spend much cash upfront (almost by definition).

There are no guarantees with equity crowdfunding. If you spend a lot upfront, but then have a failed campaign, you will end up financially worse-off than when you started. It's a risk, but nothing in business is risk-free.

I asked the founders who I interviewed for this book what they paid in upfront costs. The answers ranged from "almost nothing", up to US$35,000, with a wide range in-between. US$5,000 – US$10,000 was about average.

Professional Services

What follows is a list of what you will need to prepare before you can launch your equity crowdfunding campaign. Some of these will require specialist input, while others you can do yourself. Remember that work you do yourself will cost you in time instead of money. Ask yourself: which resource is scarcest for you – time, or money?

Looking at this list, think of your internal team and what they can do. Do they have the capacity to do a professional job? A frank assessment of which skills you have and which you lack will determine what you need to seek from external professional service providers.

- An **information memorandum** that details your business plan, market size, competitors, etc.

- A **financial model** with projected business performance.

- A detailed breakdown of **how you plan to spend the money.**

- A justifiable **valuation** for your company.

- A **video** that gets potential investors to want to know more.

- A **promotion** strategy, to get the word out to investors.

- **Legal review** of various documents.

Platform Fees

Here are the fees charged by equity crowdfunding platforms:

1. **Upfront application fee**: Typically charged to offset administrative and review costs. Some platforms don't charge an upfront application fee.

2. **Success fee:** Likely to be the largest fee, but it is contingent on success – as in, if your offer is not successful, then it will not be charged. Success fees are paid before the proceeds are given to the company raising money.

3. **Carry**: This is short for 'carried interest.' If your company goes on to be sold or meets certain other conditions that show an increase in valuation, then a slice will be retained by the platform. Not all platforms charge carry.

4. **Ongoing maintenance fees**: Platforms may provide additional services, such as a nominee account for shareholder management. If so, these will be ongoing costs.

Read the fine print. All fees need to be disclosed by the platform, so make sure you understand what they are, and how they work, before signing on the dotted line.

Saving Money

Now for an important question: *how can you reduce these expenses?* The companies able to run an equity crowdfunding campaign on a shoestring budget tend to be either:

- The 'local businesses with a crowd' with a large email list. They can generate enough interest from their own list that they don't need to pay for much external promotion.

- The 'potential big winners' with financial investors already backing them. They have received early money from large investors before launching their campaign, which builds strong momentum, resulting in other investors joining too.

Here are some top tips to keep your upfront costs low:

- Try to apply for financial support to help you meet some of your costs. Some government programs help with meeting professional service fees.

- Not all fees need to be incurred at the same time. If you haven't approached any crowdfunding platforms yet, the most important document to get done is the pitch. Only once the decision to launch has been definitively made do you need to get the ball rolling on video, promotions, etc.

- Identify where you have capability internally. One member of your team might be able to do the graphic design, another might be competent in putting together financial projections. Leverage these internal resources as much as you can.

- For the skills you do not have, you may still be able to do some of the work yourself and get a professional to finish it off. For example, you can write the script of the video yourself, even if you don't have the expertise or equipment to film it. This means less time (and expense) required from the professional. If you plan to do part of the work yourself, engage the professional early to help with directing your efforts most efficiently.

- Ask which service providers other founders used and what they paid. This will prevent anyone from overcharging you.

- Ask several service providers for quotes, so that you can compare the fees charged. Ask for quotes for a set amount of work, to get an apples-for-apples comparison.

- Ask about fixed-fee and fee-cap arrangements. Being on the clock on a per-hour basis can make you hesitant to reach out to your advisors for advice. It also leaves you exposed to the possibility of a larger-than-expected bill. It is better to get cost certainty for an agreed quantity of work.

Look for *value for money* and *quality*, not the lowest fee possible. Experience is worth paying for. If those advisors can improve your chances of raising six or seven figures with equity crowdfunding, then their fees can be a real bargain.

How Tutora Spent Next-To-Nothing On Their Campaign

"We spent pretty much zero before we raised money," says Mark Hughes of Tutora, "And that was one of the main attractions of equity crowdfunding, really. Before we settled on crowdfunding, we thought we were going to need to bring together a deal, involving lawyers from different sides, trying to put together an agreement with investors written from scratch. Whereas with equity crowdfunding, there is *one* standard set of terms that is already written that everybody has to sign up to. That made the legal side of things extremely easy."

"On the due diligence side, we spent a lot of time, but we didn't need outside assistance. We still had to make sure all statements we made were referenced, but we did all of that ourselves."

"We didn't do a video. The platform didn't insist on one, so we chose not to. Instead, we used written information only. Our promotion strategy was simple – we secured a lot of investment before we went live. Some of that came from old work colleagues, some of it came through reaching out to everybody we knew on social media and trying to get people interested. That momentum had just as much influence as a video."

Tutora is a platform that helps students find a private tutor. Mark Hughes believes this business model helped their fundraising efforts: "We have quite an easy-to-understand company, so we didn't have to spend a lot of time explaining what we do. Private tutoring – everybody 'gets' it. Then, since it was already making a reasonable amount of revenue, people could see that our business evidently works."

You can download an audio recording of my entire interview with Mark Hughes at **www.nathanrose.me/equity**

Tutora gained all the money they were seeking in just five days, while hardly spending anything upfront. This goes to show that running an equity crowdfunding offer on a tight budget *is* possible, if you are smart about it.

Chapter 3

Structuring Considerations

"We make choices, and are in turn made by them."

- Sheena Iyengar

There are many choices to make about how you want to run your offer and this chapter steps through them. This needs to come before you choose a crowdfunding platform, because your choice of platform will, in part, be determined by your preferred structure. Not all platforms offer all options.

Setting The Minimum Investment Amount

You need to set the minimum amount that you want from each investor. You wouldn't want to bother with people only willing to contribute a penny towards your raise. What about $1? Probably, still no. What about $50 per investor? $1,000? Or are you unwilling to deal with small shareholders, and only want those who have at least $20,000 to invest?

Some platforms facilitate offers with these very high minimums and still call it "crowdfunding," although at such high levels, it is questionable whether the "crowdfunding" moniker should still be used, given such a high minimum shuts out the "crowd".

Chris Thomas of Eureeca provides his perspective: "We strongly feel that equity crowdfunding works just as well for entrepreneurs looking for 10 investors to put in $50,000 each as it does for entrepreneurs looking for 1,000 investors putting in $500 each. By bringing the process online, we can enable a conversation with 100, 1,000, or even 10,000 investors in a much more streamlined, transparent, and efficient manner."

The minimum you set will have implications for the number of people you ultimately get invested in your company. If you set a very low minimum (say, $10) you can naturally expect to find that more people can afford such a small amount, resulting in more shareholders than if you had set a higher minimum (say, $1,000). Whether having lots of small shareholders is desirable or not depends on what kind of business you have. Consumer-facing businesses may favor having a very large number of shareholders for marketing and exposure reasons.

If you set a high minimum, you also miss out on the money of those who you have priced out. Not everyone can afford to invest $1,000 into a risky startup. Still, some companies would prefer to restrict access to people who have more financial resources at their disposal. People chipping in $10 probably haven't taken much time to consider whether your business case stacks up – the amount at stake is little more than the cost of a lottery ticket. Do you want these types of people as shareholders? Maybe you don't really mind, because *$10 is $10,* whatever the investor's motivations were. But raising the limit is a way of increasing the level of sophistication on your shareholder register.

Some platforms do not allow a company to set a minimum as low as $10. Other platforms do. If you are strongly inclined to go one way or the other, check what the platform's policy is before you commit to them.

There may also be regulated maximum amounts in certain countries. For example, at the time of writing in the United States under Title III crowdfunding, non-accredited investors could put a maximum of US$2,000 or 5% of their annual income into each offer. If you set your campaign's minimum above the maximum that non-accredited investors can invest, it will cut these ordinary investors out entirely.

Consider too that people who have contributed more are naturally more *invested* in the success of your business, and more willing to provide other assistance to the company on an ongoing basis.

You need to weigh the benefits of a large shareholder base against the drawbacks, and that really depends on what kind of business you have. If you want a smaller set of large shareholders for ease of management, and to keep the information you share with your shareholders more tightly held, then you should naturally set the limit higher. If you have a consumer-facing business, then there are greater advantages to having more small shareholders to act as brand advocates, and a low minimum will let you achieve this.

Direct vs. Nominee Shareholding

You need to decide whether your new investors become shareholders in your company directly, or become shareholders through a nominee company.

A direct shareholding structure means that each investor is granted shares in your company directly. It is the most straightforward way.

Direct Shareholding Structure

A nominee structure means the crowdfunding investors instead become shareholders of an intermediary "nominee" company. Then, this single nominee company holds a shareholding in the operating company. So all crowdfunded investors are pooled together into a single entity who vote and act as one.

Nominee Shareholding Structure

Direct shareholding fosters closer connection with investors, as they have more of a direct line to you. Crowdcube co-founder Luke Lang had this to say: "Direct ownership more effectively evangelizes your shareholders. Investors feel a greater sense of connection and are arguably more likely to be proactive ambassadors of a brand if they have a direct connection with the company. Dealing via a nominee creates an intermediary which can detract from that sense of connection; for example, we know that many investors on Crowdcube like the direct connection and contact with the businesses they invest in."

On the other hand, nominee companies simplify follow-on investment. They also enable more efficient company decision-making. Say that you need to pass a company resolution that needs 75% of shareholders to approve, and due to crowdfunding you have 100 small shareholders. If you have a direct shareholding structure, it might be hard to get enough of your shareholders to return their voting forms, and the company will legally not be able to act. But if you have a nominee company, then all the votes represented by the nominee company will be activated, even if some shareholders can't be tracked down.

A disadvantage of doing things this way (from the investors' standpoint) is, under the nominee structure, the votes of an individual are effectively subsumed into what the majority of other shareholders within the nominee have voted for. For example, imagine you are a shareholder, and want to vote *against* a company resolution, but a majority of the other shareholders within the nominee company vote *in favor*. Because 'in favor' is in the majority, *all* of the votes within the nominee company are swept up to vote in favor of the resolution, including yours. Some investors don't like this.

Seedrs is one platform that, as of the time of writing, insists on a nominee structure for all of their deals, and Frank Webster was unequivocal when I spoke to him: "I can understand why psychologically it is a nice thing to have a share certificate that you can frame and stick on a wall. But the reality of investing in equity via a crowdfunding platform is that without a nominee structure, minority shareholders have very little in the way of protection. Any angel investor or venture capitalist would always have a shareholder agreement in place to provide a level of shareholder protection. As a microscopic minority shareholder in a company without a nominee structure, you wouldn't have this very fundamental thing that every professional investor insists on."

The nominee structure also comes with an extra level of cost. There are professional organizations that run nominee companies, and they don't work for free, so you will need to build this extra cost into the operations of your company on an ongoing basis.

The direct vs. nominee debate will continue, and which of them is the right approach depends on who you ask.

	Direct	Nominee
Advantages	More direct contact with shareholders Cheaper	Simplifies shareholder management Simplifies follow-on investing
Disadvantages	Fewer shareholder protections Shareholder management harder	Less connection with shareholders More expensive

Private Offer vs. Public Offer

We have seen equity crowdfunding evolve from public offers to ordinary investors into a range of online capital raising solutions. It now includes public offers, private offers, offers exclusively to wholesale investors, and private brokering.

Even though the mission of equity crowdfunding is commonly understood to be about improving access, some platforms have very deliberately continued facilitating investor exclusivity, with deals restricted to accredited and high net worth investors only.

There are two reasons for this. In some countries, accredited investors receive more liberal regulatory treatment, such as being able to invest more in each offer than an ordinary investor. Also, by offering solely to accredited investors, companies can escape the maximum raise size limits mentioned in Chapter 1.

There are pluses and minuses for excluding ordinary investors.

By keeping an offer restricted to accredited investors, the company raising the funds will have the details of their raise spread less widely. The business plan, financials, and valuation of the company will not be exposed to the public. For certain businesses where intellectual property is critical, the disadvantage of revealing commercially-sensitive information to one and all may be too important to trade off against the publicity advantages that come with a public offer.

SOS was a company that opted to do their offer privately. Their company was offering convertible notes (a more complicated way of offering equity exposure, described in a later section in this chapter). "We were very conscious of having too many small investors with a convertible note. A convertible note is a complex instrument," explains Tom Mayo. SOS is also a US-based company, which was, however, doing its crowdfunding campaign in New Zealand. The combination of these extra layers of complexity convinced SOS that it wouldn't be wise to promote their offer to ordinary investors.

Your decision will also have ramifications for your shareholder register. A smaller number of more-sophisticated investors is an outcome that some companies find attractive. A smaller number of shareholders will be cheaper to administer, and easier to have a more in-depth relationship with. You can know 10 shareholders by name and speak to them regularly, but you can't do the same with 1,000 shareholders.

Remember too that running a private offer cuts down the audience that can be marketed to. There will be fewer investors who will see your offer.

Some argue that excluding ordinary investors takes the 'crowd' out of 'equity crowdfunding,' and such platforms that only accept accredited investors should be more logically called 'accredited investor platforms.' There is some sense to this, but for now the exclusive platforms have succeeded in co-opting 'crowdfunding' as a word used to describe what they do.

Ultimately, the company will decide on the best way to raise the funding it needs — whatever it is called. The accredited-only platforms are another capital raising option open to founders.

Prospectus Offer vs. Reduced Disclosure Offer

As mentioned in Chapter 1, one of the things that defines equity crowdfunding in the eyes of many is the reduced disclosure aspect. But we are starting to see the full prospectus re-emerge as an option.

Using the special reduced disclosure equity crowdfunding rules will suit most early-stage ventures. They provide the publicity benefits that are one of the hallmarks of crowdfunding, while being far less burdensome to prepare than a prospectus, and potentially imposes fewer ongoing compliance obligations.

But for the companies which can afford it, a prospectus is a way to raise an uncapped amount of money, while still retaining the publicity benefits. Having a prospectus means you can market your campaign more widely. For instance, BrewDog raised in excess of the maximum which could be raised through non-prospectus crowdfunding in April 2016. By having a prospectus, they were able to raise £19 million facilitated through an equity crowdfunding platform.

SyndicateRoom has embraced this broader definition of equity crowdfunding, partnering with the London Stock Exchange as an approved intermediary to play a part in initial public offerings and share placements. "80% of equity offers on the London Stock Exchange in 2015 didn't include any form of access to ordinary investors – it all went to institutional investors" says Tom Britton of SyndicateRoom. "A traditional broker doesn't have the means to efficiently include retail investors in a raise. But, by taking the technology for efficient private raises and repurposing it for the public markets, we open the door for retail investors to get back into these public market offers".

However, prospectuses are very time-intensive and costly to prepare. They will likely require a great deal of input from professional services firms. Also, consider the additional reporting requirements following the raise – depending on the country, you may need to produce annually-audited financial accounts or use of proceeds schedules. There may be other ongoing compliance obligations as well, including in relation to disclosure and record-keeping.

Reckon on tens of thousands of dollars of expense, just to get to the starting line with a prospectus. If you can cover this cost, by all means consider this route to enable the greatest amount of flexibility in capital raise amount and investor base to market to.

Types Of Shares

The simplest structure is to offer ordinary shares of equity. For instance, if you started with 80,000 ordinary shares, and then you issue 20,000 more ordinary shares to new investors, then those new investors will have 20% of the company – including 20% of the votes at shareholder meetings, 20% of the rights to dividends, and claim to 20% of the proceeds in the event of the company being sold.

But though issuing ordinary shares is the simplest way, it is not the only way.

Non-Voting Shares

'Non-voting shares' are exactly what they sound like. While ordinary equity holders can vote on matters like appointment of directors and whether the company will be sold, non-voting shareholders do not get their voices heard. But non-voting shares still carry with them the other rights ordinarily attached – they get a proportional share of dividends and proceeds from business sale.

On some platforms you will see both types of shares being offered: non-voting shares to smaller investors (below a certain threshold), and voting shares to larger investors. Haughton Honey is a company that gave their smaller investors non-voting shares, and their larger investors voting shares: "We did this for two reasons," explains owner Crispin Reeves, "One was that we didn't want to have to round up all the people who had just put in £10 every time we needed to make a decision that required a vote. The second was that we wanted to encourage people to invest a larger amount. We set our minimum to get voting shares at £500 – our thinking was, if a person was thinking of putting in, say, £200, then the lure of getting voting shares instead would convince them to bump up their investment to a higher level."

While offering non-voting shares may sound great (as you get to retain greater control of your company direction), remember that reducing the rights attached to shares, will, all else equal, reduce the desire of investors to acquire them. The impact this has on your valuation and the interest your offer attracts is impossible to accurately quantify, but at least some would-be investors may choose not to participate if you don't offer them voting rights.

"If a company is worried about shareholder management, an alternative to non-voting shares is to use a nominee structure," says Tom Britton of SyndicateRoom. "The nominee can collect and aggregate votes, manage the issuing of tax certificates, and handle other administrative tasks in relation to the shareholders on behalf of the company, while preserving shareholder rights."

Convertible Notes

A convertible note is a way of delaying the valuation to a later date. Investors in the convertible note commit their money now, but the number of shares of equity they ultimately receive is determined in the future, using the valuation at which the *next* round of capital raising takes place, usually with a discount attached.

A convertible note with a 30% discount could work as follows: the convertible note holders put in $1 million today. In a year's time, a venture capital firm values the company at $10 million and invests on this basis. The convertible note holders would get their $1 million of convertible notes turned into equity as though the company were valued at $7 million. This discount is meant to compensate the convertible note holders for the additional risk they took by investing in the company at an earlier stage.

International Access

If you want to access investors beyond your national borders, make sure to ask the platform whether they can facilitate this.

In many cases, the crowdfunding platform you use will need to be registered as a licensed dealer in the same country that your company is incorporated in. "Many platforms are singular, and they are not very good at operating outside of their home country," says Bret Conkin of Crowdfund Suite. "But some platforms are taking a broader view, which provides a powerful and efficient way to embrace cross-border investment."

It may be possible to use a foreign equity crowdfunding platform, especially within trans-national organizations like the European Union. "Generally, this will mean you are subject to two sets of regulations," says Anne Hakvoort of FG Lawyers. "For example, if you have a French company and wish to raise using a crowdfunding platform based in the Netherlands, then it's possible, but you will need to abide by both French law and Dutch law."

If you think there is a larger audience in the foreign platform, then this increase in complexity may be worthwhile.

"We have built investor bases in different countries and have the licensing to facilitate it," says Peter Moore of Invesdor. "That means we can try and match-make entrepreneurs with investors cross-border. It was a challenge in the past – before equity crowdfunding, if companies wanted to access a set of investors, they would have had to go there and set up shop.

Equity crowdfunding is opening up many more doors. It is not only interesting from an 'access to capital' point of view, but it is also interesting from a business development point of view. Companies who want to expand abroad can get shareholders with local knowledge who can help them to internationalize the brand. We have even seen companies issue foreign-language business cards to their overseas investors."

From the perspective of investee companies, only having access to local capital pools limits the investor audience when conducting a fundraising. Access to a more diverse set of investors provides entrepreneurs with more choice, higher valuations, and a better chance of success.

With the advent of the Internet, visa liberalization, and comprehensive free trade agreements, the old national borders are disintegrating in many areas of economic life. Innovation is now (at last!) touching the field of investing. As a force for change, equity crowdfunding will hopefully help move us toward further regulatory harmonization.

The "White Label" Option

A recent trend has been for companies conducting large raises to set up their own platform, rather than pay a fee to an established platform.

Bret Conkin of Crowdfund Suite explains it this way: "White label is a software that allows an issuer to run a crowdfunding campaign directly, without using another platform. You can take your own brand and get the functionality, workflow and compliance of a platform that you run yourself. It means it is on you to find your own investors and bring them to your platform, but you will have better control of them once they are there."

White label providers run a software-as-a-service business model. Providers vary in terms of cost and sophistication, but anchor your expectations around a US$5,000 – US$25,000 upfront cost, and an ongoing cost of around US$1,000 – US$3,000 per month. You can trade off these costs against the success fees that established platforms charge, but remember that white label charges are *upfront* costs which will be charged regardless of whether your campaign is successful or not.

Brock Murray works at Katipult, which is one of the world's largest white label providers. He sums up the proposition this way: "If you have your own crowd to bring to the raise, then using a white label provider means you can keep your own branding throughout the investor experience. It is also particularly useful for repeat issuers such as real-estate, because the upfront cost is diffused over many more raises. But if you are a startup and only expecting to be a one-time issuer, then you are probably better off with using an established platform. There are upfront and ongoing costs to a white label platform implementation, and you might not end up saving money if your raise is small. White label also doesn't give you the benefits of the guidance and support services that come with an existing equity crowdfunding platform."

For very large raises who already have investors lined up, white label may make sense. For smaller raises, it is unlikely to be worthwhile due to the setup costs and the fact you don't get to reach an already-established investor audience.

Should You Use An Agency?

One of the things you will hear the successful crowdfunders say repeatedly is that they consistently underestimated how much time and expertise were needed to launch their offer.

The common wisdom in business is to concentrate on what you are best at, and outsource the rest to professionals. If you need a logo designed, and you are not a designer, you get help. The same is true when it comes to having surgery – you put yourself in the hands of a trained medical practitioner. Successful people tend to understand what they are best at, and get high-quality advice on board when they need it.

You know your business better than anyone – that's a given. But can you explain it to the investing public better than anyone? Do you know which parts of your offer are holding you back? Can you navigate the different crowdfunding platform options?

Crowdfunding agencies come from a variety of backgrounds including finance, marketing, and public relations. There are also large agencies which offer an entire suite of services under one roof.

Whether or not to use an agency depends on what skills you have within your team, how much time your team can afford to devote to pulling it all together, and what your budget is.

An equity crowdfunding agency will have seen many successful (and unsuccessful) campaigns up close, so they know what to do and what not to do. They can guide you so you don't make the same mistakes others have. They can make your campaign better, and give you a better chance of success.

A crowdfunding agency can also function as a motivational force once you go live. Almost every campaign experiences a bump or setback and an agency can help you get through this. Crowdfunding remains an unpredictable business; you never *really* know how the public will react until you launch, but an experienced crowdfunding agency will have seen it all before.

Hiring an agency can also save time. You won't have to spend as much time learning how to crowdfund, and they can make sure your efforts are being spent the right way. With an experienced agency as your pilot, important choices can be made faster. This can save you a lot of effort.

"Our view is external campaign agencies are crucial to the process as it enables the entrepreneur to work with an expert to empower and inspire them to build out their network," says Chris Thomas of Eureeca.

What About The Costs?

Of course, there is a price tag attached to using an equity crowdfunding agency. If you are a startup trying to raise money, your resources are likely limited. So you have a choice to make; either you need to trust in the agency's ability to help you get you the result, or you need to learn how to do things yourself.

Consider the risk-reward profile: what the agency costs, vs. how much money you are trying to raise. You don't want to pay a fee which is too large in comparison to your funding goal. If your raise is small, then the fee of an equity crowdfunding agency could represent an overly-large proportion of it. In this case, group learning such as workshops and online training might be a better fit for your budget. If you are raising larger amounts, then the cost of an agency becomes smaller as a percentage of the total raised, and therefore makes more sense.

Many cash-strapped company founders want to know: 'will agencies work on the basis of a success fee alone?' Generally, the answer is no. Some will work on retainer plus success fee, while others will demand straight retainer.

There are just too many factors at play that determine an equity crowdfunding campaign's success and, while a good agency can help, they cannot control all of them. The quality of the company itself matters a great deal, the founder's willingness to put in the work is vital, and luck plays a part too. "Try as one may, it's not possible for even the most successful of crowdfunding agencies to predict the success of a campaign" is the way that crowdexpert.com put it.[11]

To see whether an agency will be a good fit for you, ask about:

- What their skill set is, and does this match with the needs you have identified?

- How credible are they?

- Why do they say their past campaigns succeeded or failed?

---

[11] http://crowdexpert.com/crowdfunding-info/crowdfunding-consultants/

Do you back this agency to save you time, and give you a better chance to make it worth the expense? Or do you prefer to tackle the project yourself, learning as you go?

Whether you decide to bring an agency on board or not, remember that you still need to take charge and commit time to your crowdfunding campaign – the agency will help show you where your time is best spent, but it is not possible to get an agency to do your campaign for you. It still needs to be you fronting the video and speaking to investors. You can never outsource all of the work.

Making decisions on these structuring considerations, or at least establishing a preference, will stand you in good stead when it comes time to open the dialogue with the crowdfunding platforms and decide on the one you want to work with. It is to this subject we turn next.

Chapter 4

————— ∼ —————

Evaluating The Platforms

"We did our homework on other platforms, but ultimately decided to go with the one we did because they seemed to have facilitated the most raises that were like ours. We assumed that the platform with the most experience with our kind of raise would be the one best placed to help us."

- Alex Zivoder (Raised £3.99 million on Crowdcube)

Choosing the right crowdfunding platform is as important to a successful offer as the choice of where to open a shop front. Location, location, location. If you are not promoting your offer where your potential investors naturally congregate, it will be much harder to attract those you need.

The wrong platform can ruin your offer in many other ways. If they don't have the expertise to advise you properly, or if your working style clashes with theirs, it will be practically impossible to create an effective campaign.

When you start looking, you will quickly notice that there are a lot of platforms to choose from. At first glance, all of them look pretty similar – nice landing pages, slick social media presence, and most of them even *sound* alike; their names invariably feature at least one of "Crowd," "Angel," "Seed," or "Fund."

You might be thinking: wouldn't things be so much easier if there was just one place we could all go to where all companies would list, and all investors could go to find them? An 'Amazon of equity crowdfunding,' if you will.

In time, we will probably see consolidation around a few larger players, but right at the moment, equity crowdfunding platforms are springing up everywhere, similar to the early days of social media. Remember Friendster, Bebo, and Myspace? Eventually all of them fell to the mighty Facebook, but before that happened, you would have some friends on one social media site, and some on others. Eventually, there came a point where enough people were on Facebook that everyone switched, and those other social media sites quietly vanished.

Due to securities law differences that make it trickier to spread globally, there may not be a single, global platform, but in five or ten years' time it seems unlikely there will be more than a few large players in each country.

When you are evaluating all the platform choices against one another, you need to find the one that gives you the most confidence in their ability to get the job done. "Different platforms run radically different models," says Frank Webster, Campaigns Director at Seedrs. "It is a matter of doing your own due diligence on the platforms and their abilities, and we would always encourage entrepreneurs to do that. Making the wrong decisions at the outset can leave you stuck with the wrong people for a very long time."

A simple, over-riding rule to keep in mind is: *you should probably use a bigger platform, unless you have a very good reason not to.* Bigger platforms have more of an investor audience, more experience with running campaigns, and a larger team that can help you with your offer.

You can email the platforms and ask for an initial meeting, or meet them at one of the many events they hold, or, best of all, get introduced to them from a well-known angel investor group or business leader. The reason it is best to get introduced by somebody the platform already knows is it will be better for your credibility than a cold approach.

Even at that first meeting, come prepared. The platform may downplay the initial meeting as 'an informal introductory chat,' but there is only one chance to make a good first impression.

Think about how you would behave if you were going to a job interview and wanted to be hired.

Show up with a clean, ironed shirt and polished shoes. Be able to explain very quickly and simply what your business does, how it makes money, and what stage it is currently at. Know the basics of how much money you want to raise, what you will spend it on, and what results you think it will have. Do your background research on the platform by giving their website a detailed read, so that you can demonstrate that you have taken the time to understand them. These are simple points, but you would be surprised by how many people fail to do the basics.

We can take the job interview analogy further. The interaction is always most productive if both sides are asking questions. They will have questions for you, but you should also have questions for them. Through this two-way interaction, you and the platform can discover if you are a good fit for each other.

I have created a form which you can print, with the questions that I suggest asking, and space to record your answers. Go to **www.nathanrose.me/equity**. Bringing this along to your meeting might be a bit much – you should be focused on the person you are speaking to, not writing down notes. Still, reminding yourself of what questions to ask immediately before you meet, and taking notes immediately afterward will help formalize your thinking, especially when it comes time to compare platforms with one another.

1.   How Large And How Experienced Are They?

Every platform will stake claim to being the biggest and/or the best by some measure or another, but when you drill down to compare the same metrics side-by-side between the platforms, you will be amazed to see how huge the differences are. If you speak to a decent number of platforms, you might even find that the biggest has done hundreds of offers, and raised multiple millions, while the smallest is brand new, and is yet to raise a penny successfully.

If they have run a lot of offers in the past, then all else equal, that crowdfunding platform will know more about what it takes to do one successfully and will be better placed to guide you. So get some basic data.

- How many equity crowdfunding raises have they done?

- How much money have they raised?

- What percentage of their campaigns have reached their minimum target?

Your preferred platform should have a high success rate, but when comparing success rates between platforms, look deeper than the raw percentage. There could be very good reasons why one platform has a lower success rate; maybe the sorts of companies they work with are at an earlier stage, and these riskier companies are just naturally less likely to fund. Then again, it could be down to an inferior ability to support an offer and see it through to success. This is why it is important to ask about the *reasons* behind their success rate – do the reasons make sense?

As a general guide, an 80% success rate is very high, while 30% is at the low end. But what is more relevant is comparing the success rates between different platforms *within* your country, as it varies hugely from place to place, due to the level of difficulty the specific laws give equity crowdfunding in each jurisdiction.

2.   How Large Is Their Investor Audience?

A crowdfunding platform needs to be able to do two things.

First, it needs to be an online place to send people you already know, and show them the details of your offer and allow them to invest. There is not very much difference between platforms in this regard – all functioning platforms have similar abilities to display offers and accept payments.

But the real value-add of a platform lies in their ability to bring *new* investors to you, *beyond* those you bring yourself. And when it comes to the size of the platform's investor audience, there is a *huge* amount of variation. The good platforms have large numbers of investors who are actively browsing their website for opportunities, and they have a large email database that can be reached with details of your offer. You should use the platform that not only allows you to reach your existing crowd, but also allows you to access the platform's crowd too.

Think of it this way: let's say you have 10,000 people within your own crowd. Any platform can facilitate reaching those 10,000. But say that one platform has 20,000 new people they can put your offer in front of, and another platform has 50,000. When you add your crowd to the potential extra investors each platform can help you reach, would you rather your offer was seen by 30,000 pairs of eyes, or 60,000?

It is not as simple as assuming that the bigger platform is automatically better. Maybe the smaller platform with 20,000 people is more of an exact match for your business, and their investors tend to invest larger amounts. Some platforms may also have strong enough networks that they can make introductions to potential lead investors. Ask about this. If they can help you find a lead investor, it will be a massive bonus.

A smaller platform will likely require you to bring your own investors to the table – and if you need to bring your own investors, you need to seriously ask: *'what value is the platform really providing?'*

If you are confident that you can do your offer purely with your own crowd, without the help of the audience that a platform has built, then you might want to consider a white label platform provider. This is where you effectively set up a private crowdfunding site of your own (as mentioned in Chapter 3).

If, however, you *do* want to benefit from an existing platform's audience, you should get an idea of the size of their investor database through finding out a few things before your meeting:

- What they say on their website about how many investors have invested with them.

- Their number of social media followers.

- Search engine ranking (search "equity crowdfunding" and see which platform is ranked the highest).

At the meeting, these questions will give you further clarity:

- How many people do they have in their email database?

- How much money does an average investor contribute?

- How many repeat investors do they have? (Those that have invested in more than one offer).

3.   Which Companies Have Used Them Before?

Only one platform can be the biggest in any given market, but platforms can differentiate themselves in many other ways.

The *right* audience is more important than the biggest audience. Your raise could be a better fit with a smaller platform if their investors have a more specialized interest in your type of company. Try to find the best possible match with their specialty and your own company by asking the platform which kinds of companies typically perform the best in terms of:

- Size of raise.

- Stage of the company (seed vs. expansion vs. later-stage)

- Sector (e.g., biomedical, consumer items, software, etc...)

On the other hand, at some point size trumps specialization. You are probably better to go with a generalized investor database of 50,000 instead of a highly specialized investor database of 1,000.

"We chose WiSEED because they seemed to have funded a lot of clean-tech and biotech companies, sustainable products and eco-friendly products. So it was a good decision to go with WiSEED for us, because we knew the investors they have are used to companies such as ours," says Sandra Rey of Glowee.

4.   Can They Facilitate What You Want To Do?

After reading Chapter 3, you will have some ideas on how you would like to conduct your offer. Different platforms have different policies on the minimum investment amount, offering different classes of shares for small investors vs. large investors, and so on. Some platforms offer a range of funding options, while others prefer to run a more standardized form that they will be reluctant to deviate from.

There is also the issue of whether your business model is acceptable to the platform. Some platforms only accept companies that are environmentally sustainable. Other platforms have a policy of not accepting companies involved in certain blacklisted industries, such as weapons, tobacco, and adult material. A company called Winner Takes All (a form of global peer-to-peer lottery) found they were shut out from almost every platform they approached because these platforms had blacklisted companies in the business of gambling.

If the platform can't facilitate the structure that you had in mind, then you need to consider how important that structure is to you. Is it a showstopper, or can you adapt your stance?

5.   What Are The Fees?

Some platforms charge an initial application fee to assess your suitability for equity crowdfunding. While this may seem harsh, more and more platforms are doing this in response to the overwhelming volume of companies that approach them wanting to raise money. By applying this initial filter, they hope to screen out the tire-kickers and spend more of their time with the companies with a realistic chance of going on to raise money.

For almost every platform, the vast majority of fees will come at the end of the offer, as a percentage of total funds raised. This means they are only payable if your raise reaches its target. If you have a larger raise to do, you might be able to knock them down a few points from their standard rate.

You should also question the proportion of the raise which the platform plans on charging a fee on. Imagine you are trying to raise $500,000, and you have already found an angel investor willing to contribute $200,000 of this. Assuming that your offer is successful, will you be charged a fee on the full $500,000, or only on the $300,000 that wasn't funded by that angel investor? Different platforms have different policies, and again, see if there is any room for negotiation.

Fees can be charged at other points as well. Some platforms charge a fee when a successful exit is achieved for investors (often several years later). They take the view that this better aligns the incentives of the platform with investors making a return on their money. Whatever the reasons, make sure you understand the full picture of which fees will be charged at which points, so that you know what you are in for.

Fees matter, but they shouldn't be your primary consideration when choosing a platform. It would be foolish to run an offer with a platform that you judge as inferior just because they are cheaper. Remember, a *successful offer* is what you are after – you would rather pay a high fee on a successful raise than pay no fee because your offer failed.

6.   How Much Will They Help You?

Some platforms will expect you to bring the offer together largely by yourself, while others will hold your hand through the process.

It comes down to how much manpower they have. The better-resourced platforms will be able to help out through support services such as web design, social media, and marketing capability in-house. They may have people who will help you with your investment messaging. They may have well-advanced legal templates that you can use to cut down on your legal expenses.

Here are some questions to ask:

● How much time they will devote to you and your offer?

● How many people do they have in their team to do this?

● What have prior companies said about the support the platform gave them? (You can track down these companies yourself and contact them directly. Most founders who have been through a crowdfunding offer will be only too happy to share candid feedback on what it was like to work with the platform that you are considering).

7.   Where Will You Appear?

Larger platforms will have multiple offers happening at the same time. Some founders think it would be better to be the only company featured, but having other offers on the site at the same time as yours is not a bad thing. Cross-promotion effects can work in your favor – the investor audience of other companies might find your campaign compelling too.

Still, something like 60% of clicks are on the first result of a Google search, and 90% of clicks are on the top three results, while the other search results get negligible traffic.

By the same token, you really don't want your offer to be buried on the second or third page of a platform. Work to understand what their policy is around getting featured on the first page, or the top of the list. It will probably work under the same philosophy of the Google algorithm: the offers which are already being well-supported will rise higher in the ranking and appear on the first page. But it is also possible that a platform is using something much more arbitrary to rank their campaigns.

8.   How Will They Promote You?

A big platform might have a big audience, but that's not going to do you any good if they don't intend to let you use it.

Here are possible promotion channels:

- **Email** – when will they send out emails to their database? It will be useful if their list hears when your offer opens, when it reaches milestones, and when it is about to close. Will your campaign have your own dedicated email, or will your campaign be one of several campaigns that feature in a single email, or will your presence be determined by whether or not your campaign is already going well?

- **Social media shares** – will they share the updates you post with their audience?

- **Hosting events** – some platforms run pitch evenings that feature their crowdfunding campaigns. Will you get a slot to speak there? How many people do they get coming along?

9.   Lock-In Effects

If you expect that you will raise capital again in the future, your choice of platform could play a part in how that pans out.

The agreement you sign with the platform will almost certainly include exclusivity provisions for the duration of the crowdfunding raise, meaning that you can't do two or more crowdfunding offers on different platforms at the same time. This is reasonable; the platform needs to be sure that if they are going to spend effort in helping getting your campaign ready, that you are not going to run off and do another offer with a competitor of theirs that could undermine their efforts.

But read the rest of the fine print too, because there may also be implications for *after* your campaign. For example, a platform might stipulate they retain exclusive rights to facilitate any future equity crowdfunding raises for a period of, say, 12 months following the close of your campaign. If this is the case, you will be stuck with the first platform you used, even if you wanted to switch.

The structures that your company will be left with at the conclusion of your campaign also matter. For instance, if you use a nominee company, then that nominee company might not be compatible with a different crowdfunding platform – again, effectively cutting down your future options.

It is hard to imagine every possible situation, but think carefully about the wider implications of your crowdfunding raise.

10.   Can You Imagine Working With Them?

An equity crowdfunding campaign takes place over many weeks featuring demanding deadlines, tough conversations, and high stakes. You should spend this time with people you can maintain a professional working relationship with.

Go and meet the actual team members that you would be interacting with during your offer and see if you like them. You want to work with people who fill you with confidence, based on their experience and background. But don't overlook the human element; if you are a creative type, maybe you won't gel with a platform that is too corporate. If you are of a more traditional bent, working with a platform where everyone is in their twenties may not be your cup of tea.

"When I met the people at Crowdcube, I got on really well with them. I enjoyed a great relationship with them throughout the deal. And, it carried on even after the deal was finished, because now I go cycling with their CEO!" says Laurence Cook of Pavegen.

The choice of platforms can seem overwhelming, but there is no better use of your energy than getting the platform decision right, upfront. The amount of variation within the industry necessitates taking the time and effort to understand the different options, and making an informed choice. Everything that happens in your offer will, to a large extent, flow from which platform you have by your side.

And one more time, let me remind you that choosing the right crowdfunding platform is a lot like a job interview. Make a good first impression, and remember to interview *them*, just as much as they are interviewing you. Make sure that the representatives of the platform aren't the only ones asking the tough questions.

Chapter 5

---~---

Pitching To The Platforms

"We are looking for companies that are really useful to customers. They solve a specific problem or offer new opportunities. The team of founders should also be competent and be sufficiently enthusiastic about their idea."

- Tamo Zwinge (Companisto)

Once you have chosen your preferred platform, you need to get your preferred platform to choose you too!

Pitching means delivering your investment story. The word comes from baseball, where one player (known as the 'pitcher') delivers the ball towards the batter by throwing it. Baseball fans will already know that having a strong pitcher on your team goes a heck of a long way towards winning the ball game. A strong investment pitch is just as important to your chances of a successful equity crowdfunding offer.

The format of the pitch varies from platform to platform. One thing is for sure – it will not follow the format of those TV shows like _Dragons Den_ or _Shark Tank_. Don't worry about being brought into a room, in front of a panel of hostile judges who are itching to tear you to shreds for the benefit of the cameras.

A pitch doesn't always start with filling in an online application form, as Charlie Thuillier, founder of Oppo Ice Cream discovered: "I was in the café underneath my flat, walking around their customers with samples of my ice cream, looking for customer feedback. One lady tasted the ice cream, loved it, and asked me if she could take some tubs home. I was just thrilled that she liked it, so of course I gave her more. The same day, I received a call from Jeff Lynn, the co-founder of Seedrs, who said, 'We need to talk.' Turns out I'd been speaking with Jeff's wife! We ended up raising on Seedrs shortly after and became the world's fastest food/drink company to reach its target on equity crowdfunding. We have since run another campaign and now have over 600 investors."

The lesson is: if serendipity strikes, be ready to take advantage.

But what should you do, assuming you aren't happened upon by the spouse of the platform's founder? Let me dispel one myth: nobody cares if your presentation slides are font size 16 or 20, Ariel or Times New Roman, so don't concern yourself with that.

The best way to *come across* as an amazing company in a pitch is, rather obviously, to *be* an amazing company – one which has *both* the big idea *and* which has made significant progress towards turning it into a reality.

Equity crowdfunding is for companies who already have traction. It is very difficult if all you have is an idea, simply because investors have virtually zero appetite for funding ideas. "The idea is such a small part of investing. The professionals want to see what you have done, not so much what you are going to do," says Peter Moore of Invesdor.

The Truth About Curation

But why do you need to pitch at all? Anyone can list a project on rewards crowdfunding and try their luck, so why is equity crowdfunding so different?

Before an equity crowdfunding offer can go live, the founders will need to convince the platform that they are worthy. This commercial screening process surprises a lot of founders.

The equity crowdfunding campaigns that are shown to the public are only a small fraction of those who apply. The platforms (at least the good ones) all suffer from the same problem: too many pitches. Bill Morrow of Angels Den has revealed that some days they hear 100 pitches and decide to accept *none* of them. Across the industry, under 10% (and probably much less) of companies which approach equity crowdfunding platforms ultimately have their offers go live. The screening process is aggressive, so just to get to the starting line you need to beat the odds.

The platforms screen out a lot of companies and only list the best ones because they want to gain a reputation for being the platform with the highest-quality deals. If they can gain this preeminent reputational position, they will stand a better chance of attracting and retaining a large investor audience, and with that, more high-quality companies will choose to list on their platform.

But wait a minute. Isn't equity crowdfunding meant to be all about improving access to capital, not restricting it? Understanding this issue will be useful for forming your pitch.

One of the oft-repeated benefits of equity crowdfunding is meant to be the so-called 'democratization of finance' – smashing down the barriers, giving investors and companies unrestricted access to each other.

But if we have got the platforms curating the deals that are shown to the public, then aren't we right back where we started – with gatekeepers restricting access? The platforms may have ditched the suits, blue shirts, and dark ties for jeans, T-shirts, and stylish blazers... but there is no doubt that some of the old barriers are reappearing.

Curation sounds good from the investors' point of view. It acts as a sort of quality control on their behalf. Those in favor of curation argue that completely open access is too risky, and that it is better to only show the public the highest-quality deals, leading to stronger confidence in equity crowdfunding more generally. But companies seeking funding lament the curation –

they believe equity crowdfunding ought to stay true to its ideal, where startups can set their own terms, to let the crowd decide.

I don't have an answer to this dilemma, but you should be aware of the tension between the idealistic view that equity crowdfunding needs to help even very early startups to raise money, and the commercial reality that it is more viable to reserve that privilege for those that are more mature, with proven business models and revenues to show for it.

Five Reasons Platforms Favor More-Established Businesses

1. **Less work to get ready:** The more-established, better-run companies are more fit for funding right from the start. They tend to have more experienced management, better governance procedures, better-developed business plans, sensible financial forecasts, and know the value of getting high-quality legal and structuring advice. Essentially, more-established companies are easier to deal with.

2. **Higher chance of the offer succeeding:** The platforms gain the largest portion of their fees when an offer is successful, so it makes sense they want to spend their limited time and resources working with companies that have a higher chance of success. More-established companies have more consistent earnings and can arrive at a reasonable valuation. Their greater traction also means they are more likely to attract a strong lead investor, or an existing crowd of their users to their offer.

3. **Larger offers = bigger fees:** Because the platforms earn a percentage of funds raised, they are naturally more interested in large deals than small ones. Later-stage companies have more need for capital and can justify higher valuations, enabling them to raise more money than startups. If you were the director of an equity crowdfunding platform, would you rather spend your limited time on an offer that stands to earn 7% of $50,000 or 7% of $500,000, all else equal?

4. **Lower risk of business failure:** Startups often fail. When a crowdfunded company fails, it is bad publicity for the crowdfunding platform that it funded on. The platforms understand that there will be some failures as it comes with the territory of the asset class, but no platform wants to develop a reputation for hosting likely-to-fail companies. By hosting more-established businesses, the platforms can develop a reputation for having the best offers.

5. **Closer to an exit:** If a crowdfunded company is acquired or goes on to do an initial public offering, it is very good publicity for the crowdfunding platform that it funded on. Later-stage companies are, generally speaking, closer to such an exit event, so the platform can expect this positive publicity sooner. Again, it helps the platform to build their reputation for attracting quality.

You should now understand the importance of pitching and be able to see why platforms undertake curation, even if you don't agree with it. This understanding of what platforms are looking for will help you to hone your pitch.

Explain Your Business

The platforms all lament the inability of founders to quickly and simply articulate what their business does and how it works. This, by the way, is a problem with startups and growing companies *everywhere,* not just those in equity crowdfunding.

As Jesper Vieveen of Symbid says: "It's very important that the pitch is good quality. We like to see a well-thought-out business plan right from the start. It needs to be clear. Keep in mind, the people at the platform who you are pitching to have no clue what the business is about at first. It is very important that anybody, even someone who has never heard anything about your company, can quickly understand it, the moment they hear the pitch."

It is best to explain your business in the very first part of your pitch; otherwise, people's minds will be too busy searching for context to understand the rest of what you say.

Practice with friends – ones who know as little as possible about your business. Give your pitch, and then see what questions they ask you. Also, you should ask *them* questions to test whether they understand what your business does and how it makes money.

If you are invited to pitch in-person, the pitch can be well-complemented by bringing along a tangible example of your product, or by giving a live demonstration.

After you have explained who you are and what you do, your pitch should include some standard sections. To help you form your initial pitch, I have created a pitch deck template at www.nathanrose.me/equity which you can download for free.

Display Your Credibility

You need to convince the platform that your company has the potential to do great things. How large, and how fast-growing is your market? What is unique about your company? What product categories do you have? Do these product categories match the actual needs of the target market you have identified? Who are the competitors? Who are the people in your company's team, and have these people succeeded in this sort of venture before?

"At each level of analysis, we consider whether potential investors will see the proposition as an attractive investment opportunity. Is the company's vision concise and clear? Is it an exciting and innovative business that people will want to invest their hard-earned money in?" says Crowdcube co-founder Luke Lang.

You also should demonstrate how far along the path to success you have already come. This is where you get to brag, so don't hold back. Have you already secured large, well-known clients? Put their logos in the pitch. Do you have excellent testimonials from your existing customers? Insert direct quotations from these testimonials. Have you received any prestigious industry awards? Make sure your pitch refers to them.

Tying it all together then, explain why your business would make a great investment. Not why it would be great for *you*.

Not why it would be great for the *business*. Why would it be great for *investors?*

But what if the very reason you need to raise money is you need to further develop the idea before it is even possible to bring it to market? Well, you will be expected to show *some* progress. The closer you are to customers and revenue, the better. Working prototypes, existing users (even if they are using your product for free), patents, and patent opinions are the kinds of things that can build your credibility.

You should also be clear on why you have decided to raise capital, and why you have settled on equity crowdfunding as the means to achieve that. Chapter 2 stepped you through the decision process, so now all you need to do is make sure you articulate the reasons that led you to believe equity crowdfunding makes sense.

"We appreciate it when people are really clear on where their business is at," says Josh Daniell of Snowball Effect. "Are they sure that capital is truly the constraint to achieving their business objectives? And if it is, have they thought through all the ways to remove that capital constraint – partnerships, grants, and other options that don't involve selling equity or taking on debt? If they are clear that equity is what they need, have they looked at the range of capital raising options? If they can show that they are clear on their business objectives, and know the reasons why equity crowdfunding is the best way to achieve those objectives, it's a big tick in the box."

Anticipate lots of questions from the platforms, and practice your responses ahead of the meeting. Above all, learn how to think from the investor's perspective and you should do well in communicating your credibility.

Financial Modeling

Too often, early-stage companies will operate for months or even years without financial forecasts. Entrepreneurs tend to prefer *doing* to planning, and it's this very same attitude of leaping before they look that makes entrepreneurs willing to take risks and build businesses in the first place. Almost every entrepreneur would prefer to spend their time driving sales, instead of poring over spreadsheets.

But to raise money, you will need to show investors your plan. And a financial model is a very important part of that plan.

A financial model is a spreadsheet which lays out your company's projected trajectory over the coming months and years. It shows your predicted revenue growth path, how many staff you will have, the cash balance in your account, and much else besides.

When you have a good financial model, you will be able to form a much better business plan. In fact, a business plan has very little basis without a financial model that backs it up – the financial model ensures that everything in your business plan has had rigorous analysis put into it, and makes sure all parts of the plan cross-refer to each other consistently.

Here are some ways a financial model can help your business. By the way, these benefits to financial modeling are just as true even if you are not raising capital.

1. **Establishes goals.** Imagine what you want your business to look like two years from now. Now imagine what the next 24 months need to look like, month-by-month, to get there. Imagine how many new leads your advertising budget needs to generate. Imagine how your sales staff need to perform in converting these leads into customers. Imagine the cost per unit of production. Imagine how much you will need to charge for each unit in your product range. Is your brain hurting yet? With a financial model, everything is all in one place for you to refer to at any time. Knowing what needs to happen across every area of the business also provides critical performance standards for everyone within the company to meet.

2. **Helps bring key people on board.** Potential investors almost always demand a financial model. But what many don't realize is that partners and employees can also be positively influenced by the presence of a good financial plan. Virtually everyone would rather work with an entrepreneur with a clear vision and a plan for how to realize that vision.

3. **An objective step-back.** The act of putting together a financial model can reveal unexpected insights about your business. You might not have realized that if you keep spending the way you are, you will run out of cash within six months. You might not have realized that to grow to the level you were imagining within the next two years, it would imply an impossible 90% share of the total market.

You might not have stopped to think that with all the staff you were planning to hire, you would also need to spend thousands more than you initially imagined on new office space and computer equipment. It is better to be aware of these things before you invest too much time or money, rather than have them take you by surprise.

4. **A working tool, on an ongoing basis.** Building a financial model is not a one-time thing. Like your business plan, it will adapt as goals are achieved, missed, or exceeded. New opportunities will come to light, your business will pivot, and your financial model will change along with your business. You will come to see it as a critical business-planning tool.

Your financial model should show the cash-generating potential month-by-month and where future cash requirements of the company may be. Your projections should also be a coherent continuation of your historic and present numbers.

Best will be to create a three-statement financial model – that is, one that links together a balance sheet, cash flow statement, and income statement. That way, you will be able to monitor your projected bank balance, which is critical so that you don't go into the negative.

It is also a good idea to build some sensitivity into your financial models, to enable you to see what the business would look like if revenue were lower, costs were higher, and traction takes longer than expected. Can your business survive under a pessimistic scenario?

Financial modeling is admittedly very hard work, and a book like this one can only scratch the surface. People spend years learning how to build financial models. It is a specialized skill set, similar in complexity to computer programming. People study full-time university degrees, and complete several years of work experience before they are really competent.

If you don't have anyone within your team who is formally trained in financial modeling, then consider outsourcing the job to an accountant or someone else with financial training.

Is building a decent financial model time-consuming? Absolutely. But it solidifies your thinking and ensures you are focusing on the right things. What could be more time-consuming than continuing to work on a business with no real idea of what you want it to look like in the future, and no real plan to get it there?

Aiming for 'growth' is too nebulous – you need to know the *how*, the *what*, and the *by-when*. These are all things a financial model will assist with.

Target Amount To Raise

How much money do you actually need? Only through putting together a comprehensive financial model can you hope to answer this question.

Your equity crowdfunding offer needs to set a **minimum** (or 'target') amount to raise, and a **maximum**. The minimum should flow from the basic plans you intend to carry out. The maximum can be seen as a stretch target, for extra things you could do. Perhaps extra money would allow you to spend more on sales efforts, open an extra office, or would simply give you more time to achieve a sustainable, self-funding business.

Remember, if you don't reach the minimum that you set, you will receive *none* of the money. For example, if you set a minimum of $500,000, and your offer finishes with investors pledging a total of $400,000, then you don't get a penny.

The reason it is done this way is investors are backing you on the basis of what your business plan is saying. If your information memorandum says you can do certain things with $500,000, then investors are supporting you on the basis of that plan, not a different strategy that you would carry out with less money than that.

With this in mind, try to set a fairly low minimum – one which will allow you to reach some significant milestone in your business development. The lower your target, the easier it will be to complete your offer successfully. Then, with a successful initial crowdfunding raise under your belt, you can always achieve more the second time around. However, you should raise enough to give you a little breathing room, so you have some uninterrupted time to focus on your business with the capital you have raised, rather than constantly be in capital raising mode.

Valuation

The valuation, combined with the amount you have decided to raise, will determine the slice of equity new investors get in your company. This valuation needs to be fair to new investors coming on board, as well as to existing investors.

Early-stage company valuation is not an easy subject to get good information on. You might have heard statements such as: *'there are too many factors to consider,'*... which of course is no help at all. As William Sahlman pointed out in *A Method for Valuing High-Risk, Long-Term Investments*, investors and company founders are confronted with the need to arrive at valuation figures, *in spite* of the difficulties.

"It is very hard to arrive at a right number. There's no perfect mathematical formula to it," admits Jaap Dekter of HelpTheCrowd. "The valuation of an early-stage company is set at whatever an investor is willing to pay for it. To get to a number to go public with, founders should speak to professional investors who are considering investing in the company and get their views."

"Valuation should be a collaborative process," agrees Will Mahon-Heap of Equitise. A valuation negotiated between the startup and a sophisticated lead investor gives others more confidence.

But even if arriving at a valuation comes through a negotiation, you still need to have some starting point to begin from. There are three main pieces of analysis you can do.

1.   Past Capital Raising Rounds

If this is the first time your company has raised capital, then you cannot use this method. But, if you have raised money before, investors will look closely at your past valuations in order to anchor their expectations for this time. Let's say that you raised money from angel investors 12 months ago, at a valuation of $800,000, and that your revenues and staff numbers have doubled since then. The new investors can use the $800,000 value that past investors used, then make an upward adjustment for the additional progress you have made.

2.   Comparable Companies

Equity crowdfunding has now been going for long enough that a good data set has been built, based on valuations achieved by previous successful offers. Scan for past successful equity crowdfunded companies similar to your own, in terms of:

- Revenue.
- Experience Of The Team.
- Business Sector.
- Scalability.
- Revenue Model.
- Geographic Location.

"Think of it as a ladder. The more you have done at the point you come to raise money, the more you can increase the valuation," says Frank Webster of Seedrs. "If you have just come up with an idea in your bedroom, that's worth pretty much nothing. But as you achieve some element of execution, then it can grow rapidly."

To find these past crowdfunding offers, you can look through the database of the platform you are looking at using, other major platforms in your country, and websites which aggregate offers from many different platforms together.

3.   Your Financial Model

Investors, particularly when it comes to startups, are trying to ascertain the probability of the venture succeeding, and the payoff that could be possible if it does succeed. Putting together a well-thought-out financial model will be a powerful negotiating tool. You can show potential investors what your business will look like under a range of assumptions. For example:

- What if your customer growth rate were to be 10% better than you currently expect?

- What if your profitability margins evolve to be 20% better in 12 months' time?

- What if a planned expansion project could be completed $100,000 under budget?

A well-constructed financial model can answer all of these questions in seconds. You and your potential investors can decide together what seems realistic.

A Word On Discounted Cash Flow

I need to mention the discounted cash flow method as well, because a lot of startups have heard of it and will be wondering whether they should do one.

In brief, the discounted cash flow method uses a company's projected cash flows from the financial model, and an assumed discount rate (which is basically a measure of riskiness) to assign a theoretical valuation.

Discounted cash flow is indeed a method used for valuing companies, but it is only useful when they are more mature. "If you are a company like General Electric, or Ford, then you might be able to start coming up with an accurate long-term forecast," says Jaap Dekter of HelpTheCrowd. "But for startups, it is completely impossible."

For startups and growing companies, discounted cash flow is of no use, because the inputs are too uncertain. The best you can do is forecast what your company might look like in 12 months or 24 months, whereas a discounted cash flow requires you to have at least some idea of what the next *five to ten years* might look like. If you currently have 500 customers, and only 12 months of operations behind you, it is completely futile to try to predict your position in five years from now. If you assume you'll have 10,000 customers, you might call your value $100,000 now. If you assume you will have 1,000,000 customers, you might call your value $5 million now. So which is it? $100,000 or $5 million? It's impossible to say. Therefore, the exercise is virtually pointless.

Pre-Money Value vs. Post-Money Value

Now for the actual calculation itself, of how much equity the new investors get for their money. Words like **pre-money value** and **post-money value** sound like financial jargon, and they can trip you up if you are not careful. But once you really understand the difference, it becomes straightforward to answer a question like this:

> *"Imagine you run an equity crowdfunding offer to raise $200,000, and in exchange, your new investors will have 20% of the company's shares at the conclusion. What is the valuation that is implied, before the new money was put in?"*

Think of the difference between pre-money value and post-money value in this way: all else being equal, the value of a house would increase if you put a briefcase filled with cash into the living room, and the amount of the increase would be equal to the amount of cash in that briefcase. It's the same with a company – adding cash to a company makes it more valuable.

- **Pre-money value** is the value of a company *before* it receives new investment.

- **Post-money value** is the value of a company *after* it receives new investment.

You should also understand these two important equations:

$$\% \text{ owned by new investors} = \frac{\text{new money invested}}{\text{post - money value}}$$

It requires a little bit of algebra to solve the question originally posed, but if you think back to high school mathematics, and substitute in the known values, you can hopefully see that:

$$20\% = \frac{\$200,000}{\text{post - money value}}$$

$$\text{post - money value} = \frac{\$200,000}{20\%}$$

$$\text{post - money value} = \$1,000,000$$

We still need to go further, as the question was asking for the pre-money value: *"What is the valuation implied, before the new money was put in?"* We need another equation which relates pre-money value and post-money value to each other.

$$\text{Post-money value} = \text{Pre-money value} + \text{new money invested}$$

The algebra here is even more straightforward:

$1,000,000 = pre-money value + $200,000

pre-money value = $1,000,000 - $200,000

pre-money value = $800,000

I have created a spreadsheet that will do these calculations for you. Download it at **www.nathanrose.me/equity**

Getting Advice

When your offer goes live, investors will have the opportunity to challenge the valuation in the question-and-answer forum, and when someone asks you how you arrived at your valuation, you want a better answer than: *'it was a number we plucked out of thin air.'*

Given the stakes, it may make sense to get professional independent advice, so you neither over-value the company (leading to a failed offer) or under-value it (leading to giving up a larger slice of equity to new investors than you need to). You can rely on an official valuation prepared by a chartered accountant, or analysis put together by someone with experience in private equity or venture capital.

Show Your Investors

"Besides having a great business plan, it is also very important to show the crowdfunding platform that you will be supported by your own network before the campaign starts," says Jesper Vieveen of Symbid.

In Chapter 4 we mentioned that a large platform will be able to provide your offer with some new investors. However, you will only gain the benefit of the platform's audience if you can generate that initial momentum yourself, with your *own* investors. Don't expect the platform's audience to carry you all the way through. If you are working with a very strong platform, you might be able to rely on the platform's audience for around 50% of the money you need, but you will still need to raise 50% from your own crowd. If you are working with a smaller platform, you will need to bring even more yourself.

If your company is a 'local business with a crowd', this support will mostly come from your customers and personal contacts. If your business is a 'potential big winner', this support will most likely come from a lead investor.

A lead investor is a prearranged sophisticated or high net worth investor who contributes a sizeable portion of the raise themselves. This gives an offer momentum and validation to the broader crowd. Having a respected lead investor holding a stake in your company will also help a great deal with their mentorship, contacts, and guidance when raising future rounds of capital. We will go into more of the benefits of having a lead investor in Chapter 6.

If you can convince the platform that you have a large, engaged crowd or lead investors (or even better, *both* of these groups) who are ready to invest in your company, then it makes the platform's decision to accept you much easier.

Red Flags

Anything that raises the suspicion of the platform or potential investors are known as **red flags**. Faced with dozens of companies to evaluate, investors will attempt to sniff out anything that allows them to instantly say 'no'.

Before you bring your pitch to the platform, ask yourself if you are going to suffer from any of these things that could kill your chances immediately.

1. Risky Reliance On Specific Suppliers And Customers

Investing in startups is risky enough. There are all kinds of things that can go wrong, but some are riskier than others.

Reliance on external parties is an obvious problem. If your business gets most of its revenue from one customer, then the risk exists that this customer might go out of business, move to a competitor, or otherwise decide that they don't need you anymore. If your whole business is based around that one customer, and they leave for reasons outside of your control, you will be left with nothing. Not many investors want to put their money into something like that. Similarly, if your business uses a particular supplier and cannot quickly switch, you could be left with no way to produce your product, and there will be nothing you can do about it.

You want to be able to show diversity of suppliers and diversity of customers. That way, if any one of them leaves, it will not represent a terminal threat to your business.

2. Immediate Need For Major Expenditure

Investors want their money to be used advantageously. Marketing efforts and new product development are the sorts of things that grow a business, making it worth more.

However, some company founders find themselves in trouble, with creditors and the tax department baying for blood. The banks won't lend to them, and they can't put any more of their own money into the business. They hope that a white knight will come to their rescue.

While there *are* some investors who specialize in distressed investments and turning them around, it is going to be very tough to run a deal such as this through equity crowdfunding. Most investors, especially members of the public, do not want their money going towards overdue tax liabilities and accounts payable.

3.   Increasing Founder Salaries

There needs to be an alignment between the interests of the founders and the interests of investors.

New shareholders are taking a big risk with you and your company. They are trusting their money with you, and if the business fails, they will be left with nothing. These investors want you to be similarly motivated to either win big or lose big.

Investors hate to see founders who want to have it both ways, and a large salary is the ultimate in downside protection. When the founders pay themselves a large salary, not only does it take resources away from the business, but it means the founders won't really lose if the business fails – only the investors will.

Jasper Versteege of Winner Takes All told me that he was living off €700 or €800 a month when he was getting started. "At one point, my bicycle broke down, and I didn't even have €50 to repair it," he reminisces. That level of frugality is probably too extreme, but being prepared to put every cent you have back into the business will draw a lot of respect from your investors.

Founders who complain they have been working at below market rates are missing the point. The entire proposition of building a business is to take a risk that may or may not work, with the hope of it being worth it in the long run. If you want to receive a market salary, shut your business down and get a job.

Investors won't begrudge you a roof over your head and food in your stomach, but there is also an expectation that you will pay your dues by living a more Spartan lifestyle while you struggle to make the company a success.

4.   Wanting To Sell Shares

Money from a share offer can go to two different places:

- When new shares are issued, the money goes into the *bank account of the company*, so that it can be used for growth.

- When existing shares are sold, the money goes into the *pocket of the ones selling the shares*, so that it can be used for their own personal expenses.

Wanting to sell shares is like wanting to draw a big salary – it means the money is not being used for company growth, and it makes investors question whether you are really fully committed. If you believe in your pitch, then why would you want to cash out?

You may have legitimate reasons for wanting to sell shares – you may want to start a family, buy a house, or diversify into other business interests. But investors don't generally want their money to be used for such things. They would rather you were *undiversified* and used every penny to build the business you are asking them to invest in, rather than capitalize on what you have already done.

5.   Large Shareholder Loans

When founders put their own money into a company, generally that contribution will be treated as 'equity'. It is possible, however, to instead treat these funds as a 'shareholder loan': as in, a debt that the company owes them.

New investors don't like shareholder loans. If a founder puts money into a company, then that is expected as part of *what it takes to grow a business*. Again, just like paying a salary or wanting to sell shares, shareholder loans raise the fear from investors that their money will be used by the founders to pay themselves, rather than to grow the business.

One of the first things that the platform will look at during the due diligence phase is the balance sheet, and it will take a matter of seconds for an experienced investor to spot large shareholder loans. Before being approved to go live, the platforms will usually insist that shareholder loans are converted to equity.

6.   Covering Up Any Of The Above

"The key thing that raises red flags for us is any hint of dishonesty. We simply cannot afford to be associated with any company or person that is dishonest. Investors will swallow failures, but not if they are lied to or misled," says Josh Daniell of Snowball Effect.

More than anything, investors hate having the wool pulled over their eyes. Maybe some of the above red flags aren't deal-breakers if the founders are very upfront about them, but any deception will be discovered. Better that you raise any potential red flags yourself than force the platform to expose them.

So there you have it. You have everything you need to effectively tell the equity story of your venture – in itself, an invaluable skill for company founders to master, whether seeking funding through equity crowdfunding or through other channels. A great pitch can be the difference between getting accepted by the platform and becoming part of the majority that are screened out.

Once you are accepted onto the platform, you will enter the campaign preparation phase. The next chapter deals with this, where you at last get ready to take your pitch to the ones who matter most – the people who you hope will invest in your company.

Chapter 6

Preparing For Your Campaign

"Luck favors the prepared."

- Louis Pasteur

An equity crowdfunding raise can be a focal point for building your company's profile. "For us, crowdfunding was 50% about the money, and 50% about the marketing," says Jarno Alastalo, the CEO of Heimo.

Because you have a campaign to do, a story to tell, and an objective to achieve by a specific deadline, your team will get the chance to pour their energy into promoting the business in a way they wouldn't do normally.

As you have heard several times now, the process is time-intensive. If at all possible, you should do your equity crowdfunding offer at a time when you have a clear run at it, not when you are trying to concurrently conduct a major new product launch or anything else that will distract you from the campaign. Your campaign should be your primary focus.

A well-structured campaign needs at least three months between the decision being made to go ahead, and the money arriving in your bank account. It could be even longer – some campaigns I spoke to said it took up to six months.

If you need the money sooner than that, then you might have to try something other than equity crowdfunding. Yes, you want the money as quickly as possible, but after you have read this chapter you will realize why it's necessary to do it right first time, rather than launch half-baked.

A smart company founder will choose to postpone or even cancel their offer rather than launch it before they are ready. The very process of going through the steps required to launch has convinced many founders that they weren't as ready to raise funds as they thought they were. Their offer may be more compelling, and their valuation expectations may be more achievable after they have hit more milestones.

General Timeline Of An Offer

Each platform has their own internal procedure that you will need to go through before your offer can be launched, but they follow a similar pattern.

The following should be used as a guide, so that you know what to plan for.

1.   Application Phase (~2 – 3 weeks)

Here you will be in dialogue with the different platforms to ascertain their capabilities, and for them to assess your suitability for funding.

You will get to meet the platforms, they will explain their process, and you will get to ask them any questions before making up your mind. I'll re-iterate that it is absolutely vital to find the platform that is the best match for you, because they will be with you throughout the rest of the process. Look for a platform that shares your values and has a track record of facilitating successful raises like yours.

If both you and the platform are happy to proceed, you will submit your pitch materials for review by their investment committee. Refer back to Chapter 5 for guidance on how to put together a great pitch.

Depending on the platform, you may be asked to pay an application fee at this point. There will then be a standard set of background checks that need to be done. These might include checking if the directors have a criminal record, that there's no concern of fraud, and that anti-money laundering procedures are followed.

Assuming there are no problems here, the next phase will be a commercial evaluation of the company's readiness for funding. The platform's investment committee will review the commercial opportunity for suitability to their investor database and ask you follow-up questions.

All going well, you will then be issued with an engagement letter, which will contain provisions which you should go through carefully with your lawyer. Once you sign the engagement letter, you are committed to using their platform exclusively.

2.   Preparation Phase (4 – 6 weeks or more)

This phase includes crafting your information memorandum, getting all statements checked off during due diligence, getting your initial investors pre-committed, and building your crowd.

This is the phase where the timeline is the most uncertain. If your company already has a good company constitution, the business plan is already in good shape, and there is no legal restructuring work to be done, then your offer could be ready to launch in four weeks or so. But if these issues need to be addressed, it could take much longer.

The other main thing that holds many companies back is their own internal capability to give the platform what they ask for in a timely fashion. Prepare yourself for a full email inbox. If you can give the offer your full attention, and address their requests the same day or overnight, then it will make a huge difference to how quickly you can go live. But if it takes you several days to respond to each request, the timeline will quickly blow out.

The preparation phase will also involve you preparing your marketing plan, which will be covered off in Chapter 7. You want to get this part right, so that when it comes time to actually launch your campaign you already have a clear idea of how you are going to reach out to your crowd.

3.   Campaign Phase (typically 4 - 6 weeks)

There is still time before the money actually arrives in your account, unless you do such an incredible job of the marketing that your offer closes in a matter of a few minutes. Don't laugh – you will hear from companies later in the book who have actually done this.

You can take as long as you need to launch, but once you have pushed the 'go live' button, the clock is ticking. There is still a lot to do – you will need to keep the momentum going by executing on your marketing plans, providing frequent updates, and staying on top of the Q&A forum. But at least now the end is in sight. Chapter 8 explains what you will need to do during the campaign itself in more detail.

One final point when looking at your offer timeline: be aware of major holidays such as Easter, the summer break and Christmas / New Years. These times have a major impact on people's willingness to invest. Think about yourself – when you are trying to get away from it all, are you really thinking about investing in companies? Most people will be too distracted to pay much heed to your offer during their breaks.

The most important times for your offer are the first week and the last week, as history shows that this is when the bulk of the money tends to arrive. You should definitely avoid having these critical periods of your offer overlap with any major holidays.

The Value Of A Lead Investor

You should also spend time during the preparation phase speaking to potential lead investors and getting them to commit to your offer. These are well-versed, experienced investors who conduct due diligence on a company, and then invest a large amount in the subsequent equity crowdfunding campaign.

The most obvious benefit of a lead investor is that a single person can contribute a lot of money. Gaining one lead investor putting in a huge amount of money could be worth hundreds of smaller investors. It's worth repeating: *spend time with people in proportion to their ability to contribute to your offer.* If one person can invest fifty times more money than anybody else, they should naturally command more of your attention.

Just as importantly, lead investors are a catalyst for investment from others. The funds they commit give confidence in the proposition to those who follow. "When you get a lead investor investing alongside the crowd, the lead investor provides more confidence to the ordinary investors that the valuation is appropriate, and has been decided on an arms-length basis," says Sean Burke of FrontFundr.

That initial money also gives momentum to the offer. "We were able to say, 'actually we have a really smart guy backing us, who understands the industry.' It's about being able to point to the smart money," confirms Laurence Cook of Pavegen.

Lead investors may also have additional networks that they can get your campaign in front of. Rich people tend to know lots of other rich people. The importance of momentum is explored in greater detail in Chapter 8.

"Closing the deals with the lead investors took a month longer than we expected. But we saw it as really crucial," says Jarno Alastalo of Heimo.

Finding that first lead investor is tough. Smart money loves to be in the company of other smart money. Once that initial lead investor is on board and has validated the investment proposition, things become much easier. But there always needs to be the one that sticks their neck out before anyone else does.

The first lead investor is the one taking the biggest reputational risk, and is often contributing the most money. Therefore, many investors prefer to follow, rather than lead. This can result in a chicken-and-egg problem, where no one will invest because no one else has yet. To solve this, seek the permission of the different lead investors you are speaking to, to tell them who else you have had interest from. Maybe no-one will jump first, but a few might jump at the same time.

Some crowdfunding platforms are very strict on the need for an offer to feature a strong lead investor in order for it to go live. Even if it's not an absolute requirement, it will definitely give your chances a boost. Peter Moore of Invesdor put it this way: "We see a lead investor as a vital ingredient for crowdfunding, but not mandatory. Still, it makes our decision as a platform much easier."

The presence (or not) of a lead investor is an effective filter from the platforms' point of view, precisely *because* getting a lead investor is not an easy thing to do. A company that comes to them with a lead investor has already been pre-screened by that lead investor, giving the crowdfunding platform more confidence to expose it to their audience, which, as you will remember, the best platforms are highly protective of.

Scheduled Pre-Commitments

Some crowdfunding companies stagger their pre-commitments on a schedule to give the appearance of continual momentum for the first days of a campaign.

Here's how it could work. Let's say you have three large investors who want to contribute $50,000 each to your campaign. You *could* get all of them to invest straightaway, so that you have $150,000 on day one. Or, you could instead ask one of them to invest on the first day, another on the second day, and another on the third day.

You could also ask some of your lead investors to hold off until you need them. Most of the money tends to come at the beginning and the end of an offer, leading to the appearance of a 'stuck' offer in the mid-stages. If you keep some of your lead investors in reserve, ready to be used when your campaign requires a boost, you can smooth out this mid-campaign lull.

What If You Can't Get A Lead Investor?

It is absolutely true that campaigns with a lead investor have a higher rate of success. But what if you can't get one – should you just pack up and go home?

That isn't a rhetorical question, because the answer could be 'yes'! If you have created the best possible pitch and shown it to enough potential lead investors, and none of them show interest, then maybe your business just isn't ready to be funded yet. Or maybe with the current business model, it never will be.

Ask the sophisticated investors who have told you 'no' for the reasons why. Do this in a polite, non-confrontational way and you will be amazed at the insights they will reveal. You might even be able to return to the same investors once you've had the chance to address their concerns and hit a few more milestones.

Still, plenty of companies have funded through equity crowdfunding, even without a lead investor. Haughton Honey raised £111,000 this way. "We didn't have a big cornerstone investor that was happy to lob in £5,000 or £10,000. Our first £40,000 all came from small investors, but we had to work very hard to get them. Having a decent brand helped a lot with that," says owner Crispin Reeves.

Here is a list of what to do if you can't get a lead investor:

1.   Be More Selective About The Crowdfunding Platform

Chapter 4 showed how many things there are to weigh when deciding on which crowdfunding platform to use. Different platforms have different attitudes as to whether a lead investor is an absolute requirement, or more of a 'nice-to-have'.

If you don't have a lead investor, and none of the platforms you speak to can help to procure one, your decision over which platform to go with will be narrowed down to those that don't have a lead investor as a hard-and-fast requirement. Then, to decide which one of these to go with, ask about their track record and ability to support offers without a lead investor.

2.   Be Ready For: "Why Don't You Have A Lead Investor?"

Don't be surprised when platforms and investors you speak to pre-campaign ask you this question. Make sure you have a good answer ready. Here are a few potential 'good reasons' (of course, make sure what you say is actually true!):

- We wanted to get the benefits of a large shareholder base, by seeking investment from lots of smaller investors, rather than a few larger ones.

- Our type of business isn't hugely scalable. It can be profitable, but the lead investors we reached out to were looking for a company that might go on to a large exit.

- We spoke to potential lead investors, but they focus on different industry sectors than ours.

- The lead investors we spoke to would be more interested at a later stage of our growth.

3.   Do More Extensive Valuation Analysis

Entrepreneurs are optimistic. That's why they are entrepreneurs – they see the future as a place filled with success under a big, bright blue sky. Consequently, left to their own devices, they tend to over-value their company.

Lead investors will bring the entrepreneur back down to earth. Through negotiation, they provide a sensible valuation under which an investment is commercially acceptable. While a lower valuation may sound like a downer, having someone negotiate a fair valuation with the entrepreneur gives comfort to other investors, and it leads to a greater chance of successfully raising the money.

If you run a crowdfunding offer without negotiating with a lead investor, you need to prove your valuation is still the result of robust thinking. Bringing in an external company valuation expert is one way to do this. Looking at the valuations achieved in comparable past crowdfunding offers is another. Refer back to the valuation section in Chapter 5.

If you do get free reign to set your own valuation, keep in mind that crowdfunding is inherently self-regulating – if you use the fact you have no lead investor as an excuse to set an inflated valuation, you stand a chance of investors rejecting your offer.

4.   More Engagement With Your Existing Relationships

Campaigns that can do without a lead investor tend to be 'local businesses with a crowd' who make up for it by selling something with high brand engagement, easily understood by the average person. Food and beverage, cosmetics, consumer electronics, etc... Haughton Honey, mentioned earlier, fits that mold perfectly.

When a campaign doesn't have a lead investor, it needs to cast a wider net and use these channels more than ever. Your best source of funds become those who already know about, use, and love your product or service.

5.   Get Investors To Commit Early

The value of momentum is fundamental to all investments, especially in crowdfunding. If your offer can't rely on a single large investor to generate this momentum, you will instead need to do it through lots more pre-commitments from smaller investors.

Critically, you need to get people to sign up as close to the start of your offer as possible. Many equity crowdfunding campaigns provide no real incentive to do so – investors can wait until the last possible moment to decide whether to invest or not, with no penalty. This is a big problem for company founders, because if all investors wait until the last minute, an offer doesn't benefit from the positive perception that comes when the amount raised is constantly ticking upward.

To incentivize early commitments, try offering special rewards to investors who back your campaign on day one, and gradually decrease these rewards for people who sign up later and later in the offer. There is more on this tactic in Chapter 7.

Writing Your Information Memorandum

An **information memorandum** is a longer form pitch that you will be asked to put together after your application to launch on the platform has been accepted. You might also hear it called an 'offer document' or a 'business plan'. I will use 'information memorandum' for consistency - whatever you call it, it is the document (or collection of information) that describes your company, your team, and the investment proposition.

As Josh Daniell of Snowball Effect explains, the information memorandum needs to be comprehensive: "With an online offer, investors need to be given enough quality information to make a yes / no decision, purely on the basis of the information you are presenting to them."

Depending on which country you are based in, and which set of regulations you need to follow, you may be forced into a very prescriptive form of information memorandum. In which case, there will be defined sections for you to fill in, and you will need to fill in every single one of them properly to avoid breaking the law. More prescriptive documents are more lawyer-intensive (and therefore cost-intensive) to prepare.

Even if you have less regulatory burden to deal with, this is still going to be a big job. No-one has ever uttered the words: *'Writing my information memorandum was more straightforward and took less time than I thought it would'!*

Of the successful campaigns surveyed, completing their information memorandum was the most-frequently cited piece of work that held their offer back from launching sooner.

Writing an information memorandum is, by nature, an iterative process between the entrepreneur, the crowdfunding platform, and your other advisors. Expect tough questions. Expect to be asked for further data which won't be easy to get. Expect a lot of back and forth. So start early!

If you are doing it yourself, expect completing the information memorandum to take weeks – and almost certainly *more* weeks than you initially imagine. You need to be able to put together the information memorandum in a form that is acceptable to the platform, informative to investors, and to show that every statement you make is defensible.

An extremely good use of your time when getting started with your information memorandum is to clear your schedule for an afternoon and sit down with a few information memorandums from past offers and read them.

Since these precedents are the finished product, they show the standard your own information memorandum will need to get to. Reading precedents will also give you the feeling for what is included, and it will get you thinking about what to put in your own. Once you have read a few, you will soon notice that information memorandums tend to be unique in content, but similar in structure.

The crowdfunding platforms will be more than happy to direct you to relevant precedents to get you started with your reading. They should also give you a template from which to start from, which already has the headings of all the various sections you will need to complete – e.g., 'Investment Highlights,' 'Industry

Overview,' 'Company Overview,' 'Risks and Mitigations,' 'Competitive Landscape,' etc. You should use their structure when beginning your drafting so you don't later waste time needing to re-organize the material.

Like your pitch, your information memorandum should explain what your business does in a way that somebody from a non-technical background can easily grasp.

To get the content aggregation started, copy and paste material you already have from the pitch you prepared when approaching the platform, from your website, marketing brochures, and internal business plans under the headings where it seems to best fit. That way, you can quickly put together a decent initial draft.

After the initial information has been slotted in, start turning it into more of a consistent, interconnected story, just like the precedents you have already read. The themes of what makes your company a great investment need to be consistent between each section. The document overall should also reflect the tone of your company culture – don't be afraid to let the personality of your company shine through!

You may be asking – how do you write simple explanations for what your business does, when it is, by nature, highly technical or specialized? It is a tricky balance to strike, but the best approach is to go through your draft with somebody from outside your company and area of expertise – an intelligent layperson. Get them to read it and show you which parts are unclear or too complicated.

Once your information memorandum is in decent shape, you and the platform will go through it to verify all the statements you make. This brings us to another important thing to do in the preparation phase – legal review of your offer terms.

The Lawyer's Role

Even though equity crowdfunding reduces the legal and compliance burdens associated with raising capital, having a lawyer to advise you remains essential.

Many equity crowdfunding platforms have instituted standardized documents, but think of them more as a starting point. There is no such thing as a completely standard offer, and every company will require some degree of customization. Experienced legal counsel can help you with this.

Equity crowdfunding forces you to get your house in order. Before raising money from outside investors, your company will need to put proper, documented processes in place, if it doesn't already have these.

Your lawyer can help you to check that the company is in good shape legally, including that the company owns and has protected key assets (including intellectual property), that key contracts are in place, and that the share register is correct. That includes making sure that any disputes or undocumented arrangements with respect to shares and options are fully resolved before the offer.

The crowdfunding platforms will want you to have an adequate company constitution (or equivalent document) that addresses matters such as shareholder rights, rights to issue new shares, and restrictions (if any) on share transfers. The platforms may also want you to have a shareholders' agreement in place. A shareholders' agreement can address matters such as rights to appoint directors and decisions requiring shareholder approval.

The company and its directors will be potentially liable for any misstatements (even accidental ones) that are made as part of the offer. You need to make sure that statements you make to potential investors in relation to the offer are true and correct and not misleading or deceptive (including by omission).

You need to be particularly careful about statements of anticipated future performance. One of the key jobs for your lawyer will be to review your information memorandum, video, and other promotional materials to mitigate the chances of making a statement that sees you on the wrong end of a lawsuit. It's also important that you stick to the script in other situations as well, including in private meetings with potential investors, and in media interviews.

Here is an example of such a statement that a founder could easily make without a second thought:

> "We will secure contracts with ABC Limited, giving certainty that we will experience rapid future growth."

Lawyers reading that last sentence will probably have just fallen out of their chairs. Notice how the sentence is making very strong statements. Words like "will" and "certainty" should only be used if you have verified evidence for them. Investors are relying on the information you give them. While you might be used to pushing the envelope when promoting your business day-to-day, you need to be more cautious when dealing with securities law – there is so much at stake, and you will be under greater scrutiny. Before you make a statement or claim, you need to ask yourself whether it has been verified as correct and whether or not it is exaggerated. It isn't always easy to know where to draw the line, but your lawyer is there to help.

A lawyer could soften the language from that earlier sentence to something more like the following:

> "We *have plans to* secure contracts with ABC Limited, and, *if successful,* those contracts will help to support rapid future growth."

A lawyer will also be able to assist with the fine print that should appear as part of an offer. What should be contained in the various disclaimers varies hugely from country to country, so your local lawyer will need to be the one to guide you here.

You need a lawyer who understands the crowdfunding regulations, but a lawyer's role should reach far beyond risk mitigation. A quality lawyer is a trusted partner who can also help with your company's forward planning. For example, if it's likely you will want to seek funding from venture capital investors in the future, your lawyer can help to structure the company and prepare the documents to support this goal, and make it easier down the track. A quality lawyer will also help pre-empt scenarios that you may not have even considered.

For example, if a company constitution is set up with a requirement of 50% of shareholders to vote, you could find yourself paralyzed by the fact it's tough to get people to answer their emails for these administrative matters. This could leave you unable to pass the resolution. It should be straightforward to fix this before your offer (and before you have hundreds of new shareholders), but almost impossible afterward.

You may already have a lawyer, but check to see if they have the right skills and experience to help with equity crowdfunding before using them. The crowdfunding platforms can also often recommend a lawyer to you. Ask about their prior experience with equity crowdfunded companies, whether they have experience with businesses in your industry, and other ways that they can support you with the offer and your business. You will eventually find a lawyer who 'clicks'.

What about the costs? There's no getting around the fact that lawyers are expensive. Still, there are a few things you can do to get the most out of their billable hours.

- The majority of the legal expenses will not need to be incurred until the crowdfunding platform has decided whether your company is commercially ready for equity crowdfunding. There is no immediate need to have complex restructuring done or a legal review of your pitch documents until you are reasonably sure that your campaign will be given the go-ahead.

- Read the templates provided by the crowdfunding platform before meeting with your lawyer and do your best to understand what they mean. That way, you can use the lawyers' time to ask higher-quality questions, rather than have them step you through the entire set of documents.

- Before agreeing to engage them, they should disclose their hourly rate. You don't necessarily want to go with the cheapest lawyer, but you also want to avoid any nasty shocks. Lawyers usually understand that startups and growing companies find it difficult to agree to an open-ended hourly rate, so ask about fee caps, success fees, and other arrangements to help manage your legal spend.

Failure to have a lawyer check off your offer is courting disaster. They have dedicated their lives to studying the law, so use their expertise to your advantage.

With the preparation complete, the boxes ticked and the offer legally ready to go, the next job is to get the word out. You need to get the offer in front of investors, and get them to invest. So, it is to the topic of marketing that we turn next.

Chapter 7

—————⌇—————

Marketing

"People see your offer here, people see your offer there. It all adds up. It is difficult to say which specific tactic worked for us. It was probably more the effect of people seeing it in many different places that was most effective."

— Eric van Velzen (Raised €175,000 on Symbid)

Maybe you flipped to this chapter first. Most company founders want to get right to the point: *What do you need to do to drive people to your campaign page and get them to invest?*

Marketing tactics are a bit like job interview tips. Anyone being interviewed would be well-advised to have a firm handshake, maintain eye contact, and arrive 15 minutes early... but these won't be enough, by themselves, if the interviewee does not have the relevant job experience the employer is looking for.

Similarly, the basis for a successful equity crowdfunding campaign lies in what is done *before* the marketing kicks off. If you have built a great company, with a large and engaged customer base, take the time to choose the right platform, create a strong pitch, and get a well-known lead investor on board, then you only need a fairly basic promotion strategy. But marketing will be much harder if you have not done these things, and need get to a successful outcome on the back of marketing alone. Good marketing depends on having *substance*, first and foremost.

The Power Of Monzo's Engaged Community

Monzo Bank raised £1 million on Crowdcube in just *96 seconds*.

Although that previous statement is true, it is also misleading. Monzo's promotional efforts really began a *whole year* before their campaign, when they made the conscious decision to involve their customers in building Monzo from the ground up.

"Very early, we asked our potential customers to help us build the bank of the future – the kind of bank they would be proud to call their own. We intentionally created a 'movement' of people who wanted to be involved with creating something. For example, when we released our prepaid debit cards, we invited people into our offices to pick them up. That way, they could come and see our white boards, meet the team, and actually give their input into what we were building," explains Monzo CEO Tom Blomfield.

"Then, when equity crowdfunding came along, it was a very natural progression for these people. They were around us so much, and felt so connected with what they helped us build, that *they* were asking *us* for the opportunity to invest."

The reason Monzo's campaign was completed in just 96 seconds was not due to any kind of marketing magic. Rather, Monzo had done such a great job of building their crowd that when the opportunity to invest arose, no one wanted to miss out.

You cannot suddenly activate an engaged community for equity crowdfunding unless you have taken the time to build it. But if, like Monzo, you have deliberately cultivated a group of fiercely loyal customers, your success is virtually assured.

Tactics To Get Attention And Money

Skai Dalziel of Guusto has this advice about promoting to the *right* investors: "Before anybody starts outreach efforts, I always encourage them to think about who the target investor is. Don't waste your time pitching to everybody. Go after a very specific demographic who will be most interested in what you are doing, and who understands the value proposition."

This section contains ten ways to promote your campaign to investors. For maximum effect, try to combine several of these tactics at the same time.

Be aware that certain campaign promotion tactics may be legally restricted, depending on which country your offer is taking place in. What is 'great marketing' in one country may be illegal in another. Representatives of the equity crowdfunding platform will be able to advise exactly what you can and cannot do in your specific circumstances.

1.   Friends And Family

"Who wants to ask their friends for money?! It is not an easy thing to do," muses Tom Hodgkinson of Idler Academy. Nonetheless, friends and family are a potential source of capital for equity crowdfunding campaigns to consider.

"Using your own network is essential, but I found it difficult from a personal point of view," says Thomas Adner of Caliente. "You want to tell people you are doing crowdfunding, but you don't want them to think that you are begging for money."

The best balance is to make friends and family aware of your campaign, but do not pressure them into contributing. Perhaps you could ask friends and family to invest a modest amount, such as what they might otherwise spend on a birthday gift. This can help your campaign start with some money in the kitty. It will also bring the people closest to you along for the ride.

In their failed campaign, Jasper Versteege of Winner Takes All relied on his family and friends too much. "It was our second crowdfunding offer, and I had been asking my friends and family for help constantly for three years – to invest, to give feedback, and to share updates online. At some point, people got tired of it. At first everybody was excited that I was starting something new and were happy to help, but the longer it went on, the more their enthusiasm waned. It was like: 'Oh, here's the latest email from Jasper, and he's asking for something to do with crowdfunding again!' There is a maximum amount of help you can extract from your personal network before you need to go beyond that."

2.   Email List

It is far more effective, and far less costly, to reach your existing email list than anyone else. Many founders already had tens of thousands of email subscribers on their list by the time their campaign kicked off.

The tone of your emails is important. You could send a message with a link to the offer page and ask your email subscribers to invest – however, this is a rather blunt approach. Just think of your first reaction when somebody asks you for money outright – probably, like most people, you instinctively recoil. Instead, use storytelling and share positive news around your company as a softer, more indirect way of encouraging people to support your campaign. Your tone should be inviting, not high-pressure selling.

goHenry is an app-based technology that lets parents control the spending of their children. They completed a £3.99 million raise, which at the time was believed to be the largest non-syndicated equity crowdfunding raise in the world.

"We didn't do any traditional public relations because we didn't have the money to spend. Instead, we relied on all the free channels: meetings and phone calls with existing and prospective high net worth investors, but also direct messaging to our customer base," says goHenry CEO Alex Zivoder.

"One of the really important things we did was send an email to our customers to ask them if they would be interested in investing, and if so, for how much. At that stage, we did not give them any more information. We just wanted to test the possible intent. There was no obligation for them to follow through, but because we did this, we had at least some idea of what we could expect from our crowd."

Emails can be prepared and scheduled ahead of time. Doing so will means that your email messages build upon each other.

Pre-launch emails should direct people to your pre-registration page for access before the offer goes out to the public. Post-launch emails should share content which was not included in your original pitch. This will mean that when you send the emails you will have something more to say beyond: *'Our offer is still open!'*

3.   Pre-Registration Period

It is a good idea to run a pre-registration period before your crowdfunding campaign officially opens.

In their pre-launch messages, Monzo emphasized the fact that they expected their offer to close very quickly. This wasn't an idle boast – Monzo had 75,000 people signed up for their waiting list. To give themselves more of a chance, anyone on this waiting list could sign up for priority access through a pre-registration period. Not only did this build a tide of momentum for Monzo's crowdfunding offer, but it drove additional users and customer registrations thanks to the buzz generated.

Once people signed up for priority access, Monzo gave the date the offer was going to open as well as the *time of day*. By doing so, the implicit message was that anyone who wanted to invest in Monzo would need to be in front of their computer at the moment the offer launched, or else they would almost certainly miss out. This generated the kind of hysteria normally only seen when tickets go on sale for an exclusive music performance. Investors were *literally* counting down to the Monzo launch.

"We did well in leveraging human psychology. We knew the offer would be popular, and we definitely played up to that in our promotion materials," says Monzo CEO Tom Blomfield.

4.   Rewards

Just because you are offering equity does not prevent you from offering other incentives. EkoRent gave all investors two free hours of driving time for their electric vehicles, while investors who bought more than 200 shares received five free hours of driving time.

Providing rewards as part of your campaign can introduce new people to your company. Perhaps the people who used the free hours of EkoRent driving time also told their friends about the experience and helped more people become EkoRent customers.

Make sure you budget the costs of the rewards into the amount you are raising. If you need $500,000 for business development, and the rewards cost $20,000, then you really need to raise $520,000, after fees.

5.   Better Terms For The First Investors

If you have been unable to convince people that your offer is going disappear in a matter of seconds (like Monzo), then you need to find another way to convince people to back you earlier.

A study by Saul Estrin and Susanna Khavul estimated that every £1 of investment begets a further 76 pence of investment, thanks to signaling[12]. Early investors signal to those that follow that your offer is worth looking at. This means that earlier investors are more beneficial to your offer than later investors.

Most equity crowdfunding campaigns fail to give investors *any* reason to commit earlier than the last possible moment. In fact, there is even a *cost* to investing early. If an investor subscribes early, they lose the option to change their mind if something better comes along. Also, some payment systems take the money out of the investor's account at the time they invest, rather than at the end of the offer, meaning they forego interest their bank would otherwise be giving them on their savings.

To overcome these costs of investing early, take a lesson from conferences which often offer special 'early bird' rates to encourage people to sign up sooner. If you choose to offer rewards as part of your campaign, perhaps could you offer one tier of reward to people who back you on the first day, a slightly lesser tier of reward for people who back you in the first week, and an even lesser tier for everyone else.

Another possible incentive is an outright discount on the share price for earlier investors. An equity crowdfunding campaign hosted on Eureeca offered four tranches of shares: the earliest investors got a 15% discount on their shares, followed by a 10% discount for the next tranche of investors, followed by a 5% discount, and the final tranche had no discount. This meant

---

[12] http://cep.lse.ac.uk/pubs/download/cp462.pdf

early investors would get more shares for the same amount of money than late investors.

Eureeca's Chris Thomas explains: "An early adoption discount is a great tool for entrepreneurs to use. The fact is, every campaign relies on momentum and early adoption. Investors that choose to commit first deserve better terms and this replicates what happens in many venture capital backed deals. It gives investors a real reason to commit today, rather than wait until tomorrow."

Not all crowdfunding platforms allow share price discounts. While this structure encourages early investors, this needs to be weighed against the fact late investors may feel discouraged that they missed out on the best valuation.

6. <u>Video</u>

A professionally-produced video can be costly, and some campaigns (like Tutora) have successfully raised money without a video. But Tutora is the exception rather than the rule – they made up for it in other ways, and had a relatively low funding target.

Most crowdfunding platforms insist on a 2- to 4-minute video. Even if the platform doesn't consider a video compulsory, it is still a good idea. "Apart from leveraging their own networks, the one thing that is most effective towards having a successful crowdfunding campaign is having a strong video. It should be short and compelling. People need to see and hear the passion from the founders' own voice," says Ken Nguyen of Republic.

It is easier to watch a video than read text. As a result, the video is the first piece of content most visitors to a campaign page will gravitate to. You need to capture attention immediately to get viewers interested enough to get them to want to learn more about your offer. If the video is too short, too long, unprofessionally done, or leaves viewers feeling bored or confused, they will click away from your page, never to return.

"For us, the video was extremely important," says Nebu CEO Eric van Velzen. "Especially today, people go for videos and pictures, rather than words. People don't like to read too much. I feel like a lot of people didn't really read the written offer information. That made the video more important, in my opinion. A professionally-produced video portrays an image of an established, professional company."

Look at the videos from past equity crowdfunding campaigns, and try and identify what makes them stand out.

"We studied several video pitches in both Europe and the United States," says Alicja Chlebna of Naturalbox. "We also decided early on what is most important for us to communicate. Our plan was to be authentic, honest, and explain what we do in a simple way. It is very important to show who you really are, show your personality and the spirit of your company."

A professional videographer should be used if you have the budget for it. Videographers are fairly expensive if doing just one video, because they have fixed costs in travelling and equipment setup. This means the cost is often not much higher if you get them to do multiple videos. Consider hiring them to shoot your campaign video at the same time as other videos that you can release as updates later in the campaign. That way, each video will be cheaper on a per-video basis.

Create a storyboard and a script for the video. Start the video with an emotional hook: a statement of the problem your company solves, and how your company solves it. Above all, make the message *easy to understand.* Make sure people know the fundamentals of what your business does and how it makes money, in 30 seconds or less. Once viewers understand the basics, the later parts of the video can go more into details.

The content of the video should be consistent with your information memorandum. It can feature images of your premises and product / service. Most importantly, the founder needs to appear in the video, in order to build trust and show the passion you have for your business. Investors want to back people, not just companies.

If you insert a musical backing or any images into the video, make sure that you have the rights to use these, so that you don't fall foul of any copyright or fair usage restrictions.

7.   <u>Media</u>

Lacking a large existing crowd, some campaigns have tried to make up for it by throwing money at expensive public relations agencies, to get their offer out there to as many people as possible. The campaigns I spoke to were unanimous — media exposure is a fine thing, but it is not worth the expense of hiring a public relations agency. It is better to be featured for genuine interest reasons, by smaller, more targeted publications.

Getting your offer featured in the press will be a matter of figuring out an angle that you can go to journalists with. A simple press release stating that you are doing an equity crowdfunding offer is not going to cut it.

"By now, everyone has heard of crowdfunding," says Charlie Thuillier, founder of Oppo Ice Cream. "To get journalists interested, you need to find your own unique take on it. Ask yourself: why should readers care about your story?"

Pavegen generates electrical power from the kinetic energy of peoples' footsteps – truly groundbreaking technology. Laurence Cook of Pavegen explains how they thought about their media strategy, "We are doing something no one else has done. We have a vision to change the way cities operate in a way no other company does. We can really lay claim to be trying to change the world, so we have an incredibly compelling story. At the time of our raise, we created a significant media moment around it, which drove hundreds of thousands of people to our website. It was a key reason behind why we managed to finish our raise in just three days."

Pavegen did all of this without spending anything on public relations agencies.

Media can extend beyond the mainstream press. Look to more specialized audiences too, such as podcasts, bloggers, and webinars. The closer the match their audience is with the sort of person likely to be most interested in investing in your company, the better.

8.   In-Person Meetings

Although equity crowdfunding is conducted online, this does not necessarily mean the entire campaign needs to happen from behind your computer screen.

You need to promote to smaller investors through digital outreach because you do not have time to talk to all of them individually. However, larger investors can merit facetime. If you can get one person to contribute $10,000, then it is just as beneficial as getting 100 people to invest $100 each.

"Before our offer, I was flying around to meetings. I even flew down to Dubai," recalls Thomas Adner of Caliente. "We were out there presenting our case, so that by the time the offer went live publicly there was a core of people who had already seen our company and had the time to think through investing in it."

If you decide to do in-person meetings, then make sure to spend your time with people who actually have substantial financial resources at their disposal. One founder shared the story of driving to meet an investor, spending an hour with them one-on-one, providing product samples, and going through their business plan in great depth… and at the end of it all, this person only invested £10!

It is hard to know how much money people are capable of investing (and it is a bit brusque to ask outright), but put yourself in an environment where wealthy investors are naturally present. Look for angel investor get-togethers and try to get invited. That way, you will be among the right crowd.

9.   Events

Meeting in-person always leads to more trust than an online representation. Give investors the chance to meet you, look you in the eye, and shake your hand.

You can organize your own event, or appear at events the crowdfunding platform hosts. Events hosted by the crowdfunding platform will probably have a larger audience, and it is less organization for you to do.

Be opportunistic with the events you attend. André Moll from MyCouchbox relates how they were able to give their campaign a shot in the arm: "We were at an event where Oliver Samwer, founder of Rocket Internet gave a speech. They invited some startups on the stage to speak, and by chance, we were one of them. So we got to tell a huge room full of people that we had an offer live right at that very moment, and that we had already raised €100,000 during the last 72 hours."

"That would have been good publicity by itself, but then we also made the comment that 'unlike Rocket Internet, MyCouchbox are actually profitable!'. The whole audience roared with laughter... all except the people from Rocket Internet – you should have seen the look on their faces. It was a pretty cheeky thing to do, but that use of humor made us memorable, alright."

10.   Social Media

This section covers both **organic social media** and **paid social media**. Social media platforms vary, but these two approaches describe the vast majority of social media marketing.

Organic social media involves creating shareable content over the long term, in an attempt to get people to follow your company's page. Once they follow your page, you can broadcast to them and engage in conversations in a similar way to email marketing.

Paid social media means running online advertisements on the social media platforms, paying for impressions (the number of people who *view* the advertisement,) or paying for clicks (the number of people who *click* on the advertisement). Paid social media is less time-consuming than organic social media because you can reach a large number of people right away, without needing to invest in building a following first. However, the money spent on the advertisements means you have to be constantly monitoring and testing the effectiveness of your copy and demographic targeting. Paid social media can also be used to build an email list in advance of launching equity crowdfunding, by directing people who click on the advertisement to an email signup landing page.

Social media is less important in equity crowdfunding than in rewards crowdfunding. Rewards crowdfunding campaigns can go viral if the product can generate significant social media interest. Social media can bring in a lot of money to rewards crowdfunding campaigns on the strength of 'shares' and 'likes'.

This viral effect doesn't happen to the same extent in equity crowdfunding. There are two reasons for this.

First, people are less likely to share what they are investing in across social media. Investing is a very private matter, so the message does not spread so quickly through shares across social media with equity crowdfunding.

Second, social media is less effective at convincing people to *invest into a company* (as is the case in equity crowdfunding), than to *buy the product* (as in rewards crowdfunding). Just think, would you invest even $100 into a company you had never heard of before through equity crowdfunding, just because it appeared on your social media newsfeed? However, if the product looks interesting and the features seem worth the price, you might conceivably pre-order the product through rewards crowdfunding. Social media is better at driving purchases than investments.

With all that said, social media will be most effective in equity crowdfunding if your company has a strong social good element to it. These projects are naturally more shareable. One reason that people share things through social media is to elevate their own status in the eyes of their peers, and sharing a crowdfunding campaign which is seen as a good cause is an excellent way to do that.

"Because we are in the business of electric vehicles, social media was more effective for us. We offer an ecological alternative, and people are more willing to share a company which does that," says EkoRent CEO Juha Suojanen. "People don't boast about the stocks they have invested in… unless it is a company they really love, like EkoRent, in which case people will talk about it with their peers. Being able to say they own part of an electric vehicle company is a cool thing to be able to say."

With social media for equity crowdfunding, focus less on the fact you are raising money, and more on the mission you are trying to accomplish. Heimo asked people to share their campaign with their friends and colleagues, rather than asking for an investment outright. They felt it was less of a 'hard sell' by asking for a social media share. Then, some percentage of those who saw the message would still go on to invest.

"We combined two messages in our campaign: our mission, which is to help people with mental health issues, and our business case as a good investment," explained Heimo CEO Jarno Alastalo. "One in three people suffer from mental health problems, so almost everyone has relatives and friends who are touched by the problem we are trying to solve. That made our campaign especially shareable."

"In two months, we sent 500 tweets on Twitter, and were really active on Facebook. We also scraped emails from LinkedIn and sent 4,000 messages to people. Some people didn't like that we did that, but it worked. Every day, we were everywhere. It made us feel and look bigger than we actually were."

Even so, Jarno Alastalo says social media was not Heimo's *only* promotion strategy: "We also contacted several large investors before launch. It was crucial to have some money already, so that when people were directed to our campaign page through our social media, they would not be directed to a campaign with nothing yet committed."

You can download an audio recording of my entire interview with Jarno Alastalo at www.nathanrose.me/equity

The lesson is that social media is better at supporting momentum you have already built, rather than being a source of generating momentum in the first place.

Digital channels such as email and social media are more effective if your aim is to reach lots of investors each contributing small amounts. In-person channels like events and meetings will support businesses which can command large amounts from a smaller number of investors.

Employ as many of the promotional channels as you have the resources to support. As Tamo Zwinge of Companisto says, "It is essential to combine different marketing strategies with good and interesting content." Use the tactics in combination with each other, and they will reinforce each other.

What you don't want to have at the end of your campaign is regret – don't let yourself utter the words *'if only I had done this, then maybe the offer would have succeeded'*.

I have created a one-page downloadable version of the tips contained in this marketing chapter, which you can get at www.nathanrose.me/equity

Pre-Launch Marketing Checklist

Together with the ten marketing tactics described earlier, there are a few smaller things to do before launch. Here is a checklist.

- Tell those who you know will invest the date you are planning to launch, so they have the money ready in time.

- Ask everyone who owes you a favor to share the campaign, even if they don't plan to invest themselves.

- Add a link to your crowdfunding campaign to the email signature of everyone in your company.

- Add a link to your crowdfunding offer on your website (potentially as a popup).

- Update your social media profiles with details of your offer and a link to your campaign page.

- Ask the crowdfunding platform to send emails to their database, and ask them to share your social media updates with their followers.

- Prepare a contingency plan for what to do if your offer is going slowly.

- Anticipate the questions you expect to receive from investors, and prepare answers.

- Assign one person the job of monitoring the question-and-answer forum after your offer launches.

Chapter 8

During The Campaign

"Since the Enlightenment there has been a very simple but widely held assumption that we are a species of thinking individuals and human behavior is best understood by examining the psychology of individuals. It appears, however, that this insight is plain wrong. The evidence from a number of leading behavioral and neuroscientists suggests that our species is designed as a herd or group animal."

– Mark Earls, author of Herd

The Necessity of Momentum

If you aren't already sick of hearing about 'momentum,' then you surely will be by the end of this chapter. But I am going to drum it into you all the same. Momentum is critical. Momentum is everything. If you don't have momentum (or can't get it), then you will not raise money successfully with equity crowdfunding. Period.

Investors follow each other. This is observed in practically every type of investment, not just equity crowdfunding.

The phenomenon of investors following other investors manifests itself perhaps most starkly in the field of economic bubbles. A 'bubble' is what happens when so many investors follow each other that the price of an asset is forced unreasonably high. People start investing on the expectation that the price will keep going up and up and up, as was the case in the dot-com bubble of the late 1990's and early 2000's.

Bubbles have occurred so frequently throughout human history, that we can safely say that bubbles are a manifestation of fundamental human nature. The excellent book _This Time Is Different_ by Carmen Reinhart and Kenneth Rogoff exposes economic bubbles of all kinds throughout the last 800 years.

Investors following one other also manifests in the angel investment and venture capital space; one thing that makes the biggest difference to your chances of securing funding is the presence of other investors. If someone else has already invested into your company, others will be more willing to.

We may like to think of ourselves as individuals, unaffected by the opinions of others, especially when it comes to something so important as where to put our money, but herd behavior is a deep and enduring part of our human nature. History is littered by bank runs and stock market speculation, all fueled by investors following each other. As the author Michael Lewis once wrote, "Investors do not fear losing money as much as they fear solitude."

In case you are still not convinced of the critical need for momentum, I am going to explain the reasons why investors follow each other in the hope that the point sinks in, so it will be at the forefront of your mind during your campaign.

Why Do Investors Rely On Others?

Imagine that investors had to make all their own investment decisions, with no way to know what others were thinking.

Under these conditions, the only way to possibly tell whether an investment is worthwhile or not would be to read a detailed business plan, and then decide for themselves whether they trust what is inside. Yes, investors *should* do this, but the reality is, most do not. Many people are not financially trained, and thus lack the skills to read business plans properly – they don't understand a balance sheet, they don't know how to evaluate markets, strategies, and risks. And even if they do have the skills, they might not have the motivation – reading business plans is time-consuming, and, frankly, not very enjoyable for most people. Doing all of this is also overly burdensome if an investor is only weighing up putting in a small amount, like $100 or so.

Then there's the not-small matter of valuation – trying to determine a fair value for a company whose prospects are based on the unknowable future. Even the experts freely admit that valuation is difficult and subjective, even for them. Equity analysts at big Wall Street firms have university training, years of experience, and go through rigorous professional accreditation, and are *still* frequently wrong about their prognostications about company value.

To make matters worse, evaluating investments is not something investors are asked to do just once. They are faced with dozens to evaluate, and they need to choose between them and do so in a timely fashion. And let us not forget, people are busy. They have full-time jobs to hold down, and lives to live. The vast majority of people making direct investments are doing so in their spare time.

Faced with this kind of challenge, investors do a very natural, very human thing: they look for a shortcut. They look to the opinions of others, effectively outsourcing the mental work that they don't want to do themselves.

Is This A Good Thing Or A Bad Thing?

At an emotional level, no one likes the idea that they move in a herd-like manner. The word 'herd' brings up visions of farm animals like sheep, and we like to think of ourselves as a bit smarter than that.

But following the crowd might just be the smartest thing we could do. Crowds may have wisdom. The entire equity crowdfunding industry is predicated on this notion – that we can take investment choices out of the hands of the professional investor classes, and instead turn this authority over to the masses to invest directly in projects they consider worthy.

The Wisdom of Crowds by James Surowiecki is frequently cited in support of the 'wise crowd' point of view. However, one of Surowiecki's central requirements for a wise crowd is _independence_. Independence means people form opinions in isolation, without influence from those around them. The fact that anyone can see, via the progress bar, whether a crowdfunding campaign is already well-backed or poorly-backed means investors are not making decisions in isolation.

But just because decisions are not being made in isolation does not _necessarily_ mean decisions are being made irrationally. Whether crowds are wise or foolish depends on whether the crowd is following smart initial investors.

If the initial investors:

- Are skilled;
- Have decided to invest for rational reasons; and
- Have done so on an arms-length basis,

Then the new investors will be following a rational decision. In this case, the fact a project has had sophisticated investors has real information content, which investors can indeed put some reliance on and reasonably follow.

Why Is This Important For Equity Crowdfunding?

A lack of momentum is one of the most frequent equity crowdfunding mistakes. If your offer starts with nothing, chances are high that it will stay right there at zero. If it's still at zero (or close to it) a week after launching, your offer is effectively already dead in the water, regardless of whether it nominally has another few weeks still to run.

If a new investor sees that others have already invested in a company, then they will assume there must be a good reason for that. *"Thank goodness others have decided which of these options are worthy of investing in, so that I don't need to,"* is the relieved cry of the subconscious mind.

Think of arriving in a new town, where you find two cafés side-by-side. One is all but empty, with bored baristas hunched over the counter, with nothing to do but check their phones. The other café is bursting with the chatter of patrons, cups of coffee being imbibed at every table, and a line of people waiting to be served by the frantic staff.

Without needing to even check the menu or step foot inside, our instinct is to assume that the empty café must be inferior… and best of all (for our lazy minds), we don't even need to expend mental energy to figure out why. Most people will be inclined to follow the crowd and join the line at the busy café.

In equity crowdfunding, crowd dynamics manifest itself through a seemingly minor part of the campaign page: the progress bar. This little tool shows how much money a company intends to raise, and how much they have already got committed. Would-be investors get complete transparency over how the crowd is moving. This sort of information is irresistible for human minds, hungry as they are for shortcuts.

People use the progress bar as an initial screen. The first thing they do is look for the companies that look like they have a good chance of succeeding, and *then* they look at the rest of the pitch. No investor wants to waste their time researching and analyzing something that doesn't look like it will even reach the funding goal.

What Does This Mean For Your Campaign?

There always needs to be a first investor of an equity crowdfunding campaign – someone who will take the leap of faith, even when no one else has yet. That special person who will stand up and say, *"Yes. I will support you, because I believe in what you are doing."*

Once that first investor has committed, it becomes easier and easier to secure new ones. Momentum kicks in. To use human psychology to your advantage in equity crowdfunding, you need to build momentum.

The 80/20 rule applies. Spend 80% of your energy getting those initial 20% of investors on board. Launch with as much of your offer already done as possible. Make it look like reaching your target is a fait accompli.

If there is a celebrity or a heavy-hitter in the investment world among these initial investors, then so much the better. People will naturally follow a known leader even more willingly. Make sure everybody knows who has already backed you. This social proof is extremely powerful.

To convince those crucial first investors is the hard part. But once you have done that and can show that critical momentum, your offer will be working *with* the tide of human nature.

How goHenry Generated Incredible Momentum

"The dozens of entrepreneurs we spoke to for advice stressed the importance of getting some initial investors on board to show momentum. After all, nobody wants to be the first. Those who had previously raised funds using equity crowdfunding platforms told us that if we could launch to the public with 25%, or 30% of the raise already done, then we would be in very good shape. We took that advice to heart," says goHenry CEO Alex Zivoder.

"What we did was break it into three stages: in the first stage, we went out to our existing investors to generate that initial momentum. That got us to 43% of our target. Next, we opened it up to our existing users for 48 hours before showing it to the public. We got great uptake from that – by the time we opened it to the public, we were already above our target – so when people had told us 25% or 30% would be good enough to see momentum kick in – well, let's just say we knocked that out of the park! On day one, the public could already see we had achieved our target."

The goHenry offer was wildly successful because of momentum, and the steps they took to generate it. By accessing their initial investors first, their existing customers could see they had already raised some of the money. By going out to their existing customers next, the rest of the public could see they were already overfunded. In the end, without doing any traditional media outreach, they were able to collect nearly £4 million.

Supporting Your Campaign Post-Launch

If you do a good enough job of the pre-launch, then your work is done! Your campaign will be over extremely quickly. But if you need to keep pushing while the campaign is open, then you still have a solid amount of work ahead of you.

Besides the marketing tactics from Chapter 7, there are two main things you need to do during the offer period: provide frequent campaign updates, and answer questions posed to you in the forum. Doing these two things well will keep your momentum going.

1.   Frequent Updates

Investing is often more emotional than analytic, and the best emotion to inspire is urgency. One way to do this is to provide frequent updates that show your rapid progress towards your target. When your campaign hits 25% complete, 50% complete, 75% complete, and heads into overfunding are all good points at which to update your crowd to show off how well your offer is going.

Of course, the only way to make this believable is to actually *have* rapid progress towards your target. A message saying: *'Our offer is going fast! Come quickly or you might miss out!'* is not going to work if your offer has been stuck on 5% for two weeks. It could even work against you, as people will lose trust and stop paying attention if you are saying something patently untrue. Don't be like the boy who cried wolf.

Another great way to update your crowd is to release positive news related to your business, which builds on your pitch. Announce new clients, new hires, new stores – anything to show that your company is not sitting still during the offer. It also gives you something to say when you are blasting out all these messages, beyond: *'check out our company and invest!'* You can get these news releases ready pre-launch.

Guusto did their updates through video. This is more relatable, as people can see you and hear you. Because video is more shareable, it can also get you more online exposure.

CropLogic sent a media release part way through their offer regarding the appointment of advisors in relation to an initial public offering. Their pitch had said they were going to take steps towards an initial public offering – so when partway through the offer, people could see that they weren't even going to wait for the offer to close in order to fulfil this promise, it was very well-received. Very smart campaigning.

2.   Answering Questions

One founder woke up on the morning after his campaign launched to an inbox of 135 new emails from people requesting business plans and financial forecasts. You ought to plan for some disruption to the ordinary course of business. There will be a lot of people who want to talk to the founders of the company, and you have to make time to do it. Best will be to assign this task to one person within the team, so that the responsibility of answering incoming questions is clear.

The question and answer forum is underestimated by many. This is the part of your campaign where anyone can ask the founders a question, and where everyone can view both the question and the founder's reply. Platforms all emphasize how crucial it is to answer questions *as quickly as possible*. If the founders aren't on top of the forum, it can damage the offer. Investors will be wondering why their questions are taking so long to be answered. Is the company hiding something? Or are those in charge just too lazy to bother replying? Both are bad.

goHenry set an internal goal that every question would be answered within six hours. Alex Zivoder explains why: "We think a lot of campaigns make a mistake by not giving immediate and effective attention to the questions raised on the forum. Because we answered every question quickly, and in full, the entire atmosphere of the forum became supportive."

Make sure that you actually *answer* the questions. Some founders have a tendency to deflect difficult questions by citing 'commercial sensitivity' – but if an investor asks a question, it's because they want an answer! A non-answer is just as bad as no answer – even if it is a hard question, or if it is a question that you would prefer didn't come up.

To show what I mean, here is an example of a possible question from an investor, along with both a bad answer, and a good answer.

Question: "Your valuation seems high. How did you decide it?"

- **Bad Answer**: "We arrived at our valuation by carefully considering what seems reasonable."

- **Good Answer**: "We looked at a set of five past equity crowdfunding companies at a similar stage of business development, in a similar industry, from the past 24 months. We believe we are more developed than ABC Limited, and less developed than XYZ Corp. We have better margins than LMN Inc., but unlike them this is our first time raising capital. Given all of this, we believe it is reasonable to place our own valuation somewhere in the middle."

You may also get questions that have already been addressed elsewhere, revealing that the questioner has not read everything you spent so long putting together before coming to the forum. You might feel like curtly saying: 'See page 12 of our business plan for the answer to this.' But don't.

Even if the questioner seems like a hostile and unfair interrogator, you still need to answer their questions politely, with utmost professionalism, and in full – even if you clench your teeth as you do so. Remember, everyone on the forum gets to read your reply, not just the one who posed the question.

I have prepared a list of common questions you might get in the forum, so that you can start preparing answers, even before your campaign goes live. That way, you will be as prepared as you can possibly be for what your potential investors could ask. Download this list at **www.nathanrose.me/equity**

Panic Stations: What If Your Offer Is Failing?

I have preached the need to get your offer right before launch, and shared lots of ways to do this. So hopefully, you will not find yourself in the position where you have a failing campaign on your hands. But what if you need to rescue an offer, after it has already launched?

Truthfully, it is going to be much tougher to change your campaign after going live, because many of the most important aspects cannot be altered. You can't change your crowdfunding platform, and it's going to be very difficult to run around changing other things on the fly, while the clock is counting down.

Many of your potential investors will have already gone to your offer page and seen your lack of traction. It is going to be hard to get them to come back if the last time they looked, you didn't look like you had much hope of success.

But if you are in charge of a failing campaign, a lecture on what you should have done differently before launching is the last thing you want to hear. It is like experiencing a computer crash, losing the progress you have been working on, then calling technical support and having them smugly tell you: *you should have backed up your work more regularly.* True, but also completely unhelpful in getting yourself out of the hole you find yourself in at this moment.

What you really need, right now, are ideas for how to turn things around.

1. Analyze Why Your Offer Is Doing Poorly

If your offer is failing, it might be tempting to respond by spending more on public relations and advertising. But first, you should take a step back and work to understand whether getting more eyeballs to your offer page is really the issue.

The platform should be able to give you the statistics on the number of people coming to your campaign page for the days it has already been live. Look at these numbers, and then ask: does your campaign need more traffic, or is the problem more to do with converting visitors into investors?

If you already have enough people coming to your campaign page, but they don't like what they see once they are there, then spending money to drive more people to the page will not be helpful. In fact, it will leave you even worse off, because of the additional expense. Don't throw good money after bad.

Once you have identified the most important source of the problem – traffic, or conversion — you will be much better placed to know what to do next.

2. Find Out What Is Already Working Best

Look at the day-by-day amount of money committed, and try to match this with your outreach activities. Did you get a spike of money committed on the day you posted a new video update? What about when the crowdfunding platform mentioned your campaign in their email? Or was it when you were featured in the local news? Whatever is working best, try to do more of it.

3. Try Other Outreach Channels

Chapter 7 advised that it is best to try as many outreach channels as possible, because different crowdfunding campaigns have been successful with different methods. But perhaps you skipped a few and thought to yourself: *'this wouldn't work for us.'* Well, now is the time to revisit the list and try the outreach tactics that you haven't already tried.

You might be surprised that when you try a new tactic, it makes all the difference. There is a multiplier effect of using many tactics at the same time. They can reinforce each other and make each of them stronger than when used alone.

4. Call In Some Of Your Reserve Money

In Chapter 6, I mentioned the merits of keeping a few of your large investors in reserve, instead of asking every single one of them to commit on day one. Nathan Lawrence, CEO of Heyrex, says that their campaign employed this to good effect. "We asked some of the parties who we knew were going to invest to hold off, so that we had a bit of money that we could deploy at times our campaign required momentum."

If your campaign is going slowly, then now is the time to call in the reinforcements that you have up your sleeve. Then, other people visiting your page will see that the amount raised is still ticking upward, and is not stuck.

5.   Ask The Platform To Give You A Boost

In Chapter 4, you were advised to get a commitment from the crowdfunding platform on what they would do to help promote your offer. Well, now is the time to see if they are good to their word. Ask if they can mention your campaign in their email dispatches, arrange a new webinar, or appear at an upcoming investor meeting of theirs. They may have other ideas too.

Platforms are more inclined to promote campaigns that are already succeeding, rather than those which are not doing so well, because they want to be sharing messages of success with their audience, rather than sharing needy campaigns. But that should not stop you from asking for help from your partners at the platform. Remember, they want to see your offer succeed too.

6.   Extend The Offer

You might be able to get an extended deadline from the platform. When you have more time, it gives investors more of a chance to see your offer. However, extending is only a reasonable tactic if it is realistic that more time would actually help. If your offer has already raised 80% of the money you need, then maybe an extra week or two to corral investors to your page could see you get over the line. But if you are only 5% of the way to your target, then the need for more time is not your problem – something else needs to change.

7.   Change The Offer Terms

Once the offer is launched, it may be possible to change the terms of the offer itself to make things more attractive to investors. Changes to your offer after it has been launched are naturally more difficult to justify, as it gives your campaign a whiff of desperation. But if you are reading this section, you probably *are* desperate. If it looks like your campaign is headed for failure anyway, you might as well give it your best shot to turn things around.

A warning: significant changes to your campaign after launch could be restricted or illegal, depending on which regulations you are governed by. Sandi Gilbert, a Canadian crowdfunding advocate, points out that post-launch changes under Canadian law would require the campaign to be pulled down entirely, new documents filed, and starting the whole campaign from scratch – including refunding all the money that investors have committed so far. Ask the platform you are working with whether changes after the campaign has launched are possible. If there are legal barriers to post-launch changes, it is even more reason to get the terms of the offer right before launch.

The question and answer forum is a gold mine for objections, and you can probably recall what people didn't like about your company from personal meetings too.

Haughton Honey were struggling in their campaign on Crowdcube until they made a change to the reward they offered to their larger investors. "Mid-campaign, we decided that anyone who invested £1,000 or more would get a lifetime

193

supply of honey," says Haughton Honey owner Crispin Reeves. "This really struck a chord with people. We saw an incredible influx of new investors who all invested exactly £1,000. We also saw a lot of investors who had committed smaller amounts bring their investment up to that £1,000 level."

It may also be possible to change your company valuation in the middle of your offer. Jesper Vieveen of Symbid says, "It is much better to get your valuation right before launching, but if the market is telling you that the valuation you are asking for is too high, then at some point you need to listen to that feedback."

Dropping your valuation mid-offer can come across as very desperate, because it is effectively acknowledging that your company isn't worth what you were originally asking for. So if you do this, then your messaging to the crowd surrounding the move must be formulated correctly – above all, people appreciate honesty. Dropping your valuation mid-offer is a last resort (and some crowdfunding platforms do not even allow it), so do not take the decision lightly, and try everything else first.

Time spent understanding whether your campaign page needs more people to see it or a better experience once they are there, analyzing the return from your different outreach efforts, and listening to what investors are saying can help *any* campaign.

Being available during the offer period is important, and keeping your crowd informed will help maintain the momentum you generated during your launch.

Expect to go through the entire spectrum of emotions during your campaign. Expect the days to be stressful, especially if it looks like it will be a close-run thing.

In the end, your offer will have either succeeded or failed, and you need to be prepared for both outcomes. The following chapter goes into what happens next.

Chapter 9

After The Campaign

"I never lose. I either win or learn."

– Nelson Mandela

You have just come through a monumental effort.

If you have succeeded, congratulations!

Some people would say you should not rest on your laurels, but I think you should - just for a moment. If you are always rushing through life, you never get the chance to stop and savor the view. Send a note to your investors of heartfelt thanks. Let them share in your celebration.

The money will be transferred to your account (minus fees), and your shareholder register will be updated to reflect the ownership rights your new investors now hold in your company.

But soon you will need to get back to work. You have made a lot of very big promises to a lot of people, and they have trusted you with their money. A weighty responsibility now rests upon your shoulders. You have got to use their capital to do what you said you were going to do.

Communication

Many companies have hesitated from pursuing equity crowdfunding because they assume the task of managing all of their new shareholders will be a huge distraction from running their business, particularly if they set a low minimum investment amount. They have nightmares of spending all their time answering emails and fielding calls from each and every shareholder as they demand constant updates about how the business is performing.

Yes, there will be *some* additional shareholder management to do, but the fear does seem to be overblown compared to the reality. The companies that have been through crowdfunding that I spoke to all agreed that as long as you are proactive in your communication, investors won't be wasting your time with frivolous inquiries. It is when the updates aren't coming that investors will start to worry and probe.

Another point: if you are really serious about generating 'engagement' with your customers and stakeholders, then engagement needs to be a two-way street. You can't expect your new shareholders to be engaged with you, by being fiercely loyal brand advocates for your company, if you aren't willing to be engaged with them in return. Do not put up barriers to being contacted. By making yourself easily reachable, you will hear the ideas and advice of a multitude of people with an interest in seeing your company succeed. That kind of crowd-sourced wisdom is gold, even if you have to take some time out of your day to hear it.

Investor updates should take place at least every three months. You should also send a longer, annual update, in line with the end of the financial year. You can do this with an email, but it will be more secure to create an online portal where investors can log in with a password and access the reports. Emails have a habit of being forwarded. Emails could find their way to the media, or to competitors, for example.

These investor updates should include an update on business performance, staff movements, and commentary on how you are tracking against the plans you outlined at the time of your crowdfunding offer. People understand that things won't pan out exactly as you forecast, and that business naturally moves in different directions than planned. This is fine, just explain the reasons why.

You can also use your investor communication to poll your shareholders to get their feedback on a multitude of things. You might ask for their input on a new logo, or a new product you are thinking of launching. You might also ask them if they have any contacts that could be useful as you expand to a new market. This is where the real benefit of the crowd, beyond the money, comes to the fore. Make sure you take advantage of it.

Delivering on Expectations

Remember those projections you made in your financial model? Now you have got to do your best to deliver on them. You will have made statements saying that by a certain future date, you expected to grow revenue to a certain level. Well, pretty soon that date is going to roll around and your new investors are going to be wondering whether you achieved your goal or not.

If you meet, or exceed, those expectations, then things are easy. You will be able to proudly trumpet your achievement to your happy shareholders. But what if you miss your projections? The natural response is to go into your shell and hope no one notices. But they *will* notice, and silence is the worst possible response.

Equity investors knew all along that they were taking a risk when they invested, and they knew things might not go to plan. Ultimately, what people appreciate most is honesty and integrity. If there is bad news, it's better to share it along with your plan for what you are going to do about it.

Your Next Round

If you have done a good job with your first equity crowdfunding raise, you can leverage this if you want to do a second raise. But it requires you to have shown respect to your shareholders from your first offer. This means communicating with them, and delivering on expectations.

If you can show your investors that since the last time you went to them, you have progressed and delivered on expectations, and they feel like you have done a good job of communicating with them, then you can count on a good number of them to support you a second time.

But if it seems like your business hasn't progressed much, it will feel to them that you are just asking them to throw money into a black hole. And if you have been silent since the last time you asked them for money, then you cannot expect them to be receptive. Don't be like the relative in your family who only contacts you when they need something. Nurture your new community by giving generously before you ask them to do something for you.

You might also choose to raise money through a different channel, such as through venture capital, and here is where the work you did with your lawyer from Chapter 6 is going to pay off. Since you had the foresight to make sure that your company structure could accommodate different funding options, you will be well placed.

The Exit

In investment parlance, an **exit** refers to an eventual sale of shares. It is the dream of the investors in potential big winners, who are putting money into your business with the expectation of eventually getting more out in the future. If you marketed your company as a candidate for eventual exit, then your investors will want to be kept informed about the steps you are taking to achieve that.

Investments in private companies tend to be difficult to sell until there is a liquidity event that makes the shares more easily able to be sold. But even in the absence of one of these, investors are usually able to sell by way of private agreement, should they find a willing buyer.

The most likely liquidity event will see the crowdfunded shares being bought out by a financial buyer (such as a venture capital or private equity firm) or a trade buyer (such as a competitor, a supplier, or a customer). It could also be possible that your company could grow to the point where it could do an initial public offering on a stock exchange.

So far, there have only been a handful of equity crowdfunded companies go on to successful exits. One is Foodist, which funded on the German-headquartered platform Companisto before being bought out by Ströer.[13]

Asked why we haven't seen more successful exits, Sandi Gilbert (a Canadian crowdfunding advocate) believes there are two reasons: "For one thing, a lot of crowdfunded companies are never going to be of interest to financial buyers. They are local businesses, but are never going to be able to generate returns that will interest venture capital. For another thing, the space is still very new. The typical life cycle of a venture capital fund is around 7 – 10 years, and equity crowdfunding just simply hasn't been around that long."

Hopefully we will see more successful exits as equity crowdfunding matures.

---

[13] http://www.crowdfundinsider.com/2016/08/88937-crowdfunding-companisto-foodist-sold-stroer/

What If Your Offer Failed?

If you follow the advice in this book, I think you stand a great chance of running a successful offer, but it would be foolish to discount the possibility that things won't go smoothly.

What do you do if you craft a strong campaign strategy, nail your pitch, go live on the platform of your choice, build a professional offer page, and launch with good momentum and then... nothing? Your offer doesn't catch fire. Investors aren't enthused by what they see. The progress bar remains stubbornly stuck well below your target amount, and no matter how many times you refresh the page, it stays there. You try everything in Chapter 8 to restart things, but nothing works.

Sometimes, it's just not meant to be.

The truth of equity crowdfunding is: not every company will get funded. "There will always be some campaigns that fail because the crowd, in its wisdom, reject them," says Frank Webster of Seedrs. "That is the intelligence of the crowd, and failed offers are part of a well-functioning equity crowdfunding marketplace."

The fact that 'some offers need to fail' will not make you feel any better, if you are in charge of one of them. No crowdfunding effort sets out to fail. The first reaction will likely be to blame yourself, or those around you. Yes, things could have gone differently, but what you really need now is a plan for what to do next.

Whatever hurt you may be feeling, you must show a brave face to the world. People tend to respect and even admire those who try, fail, and face their failure with dignity. However, those who fail and point the finger at others may gain pity, but they are more likely to burn bridges and invite scorn. Your reputation will be best enhanced if you take the setback in your stride and press on regardless.

The ones who did back you should be thanked for being willing to support you, even if you didn't make it. Many of these people will remain your customers. Others may have ideas for what you should do next. Seeing your campaign fail, and seeing your determination to carry on in spite of it all, may even strengthen their loyalty to you.

A failed offer will have taught you a great deal. You will have gone through an intensive process, with potential investors challenging your business model. You will have upped your game in promoting your company. You will have tried many things – some of which worked, and some of which didn't.

Ask the crowdfunding platform for a post-mortem into what happened. Ask them to be brutally honest with you about why things went wrong. If they think you didn't work hard enough, or overvalued your company, you need to hear it. Rather than take it personally, listen to what they are saying – it is some of the most honest, useful feedback you will ever hear.

Write down the lessons. In the months and years to come, I guarantee you will wish you had made a record of the entire experience, and all the learnings. As they say: *the shortest pencil is longer than the longest memory.*

Maybe it wasn't the fault of the platform, or your strategy, or the effort you put in – maybe your business just wasn't worthy of investment at this time. Take the time to look at what milestones your business may need to reach to secure investment in the future and, indeed, reconsider whether you need investment at all. Now is a great time for deep introspection to decide where to go from here.

If you decide you still need funding to progress, the process will have left you well-prepared to try through other means.

"While it's obviously disappointing for any business that doesn't reach its target, it doesn't necessarily mean it's the end of the road. Businesses can review their position to identify where they may have gone wrong or areas they need to improve on. Once those issues have been addressed, there is nothing to stop them from trying to raise finance again," advises Crowdcube co-founder Luke Lang.

"My advice for any business that has failed with equity crowdfunding would be to go back to basics and consider what investors are looking for in an investment opportunity and try and tick as many of those boxes as possible."

Maybe it will be as simple as taking the information memorandum you have already prepared for your crowdfunding offer to a new group of investors. Maybe you just need to tweak your valuation. Refer back to Chapter 2 for the full list of other funding options to explore.

Even if all other funding options are closed to you, you aren't defeated. It may take you longer to get where you want to go, but building a business through bootstrapping is an entirely legitimate way to go about things. Rather than hire an extra salesperson, you can be more targeted with the sales resources you already have. Rather than building a new physical factory, you can contract out the manufacturing. Rather than pay an advertising agency for promotion, you can find smart, inexpensive ways of using digital marketing to drive traffic to your website. Constraint builds creativity.

Jasper Versteege has run two equity crowdfunding campaigns – one of which succeeded, and one of which failed. This makes him very well placed to comment on both outcomes. In 2014, Winner Takes All raised €80,000 on FundedByMe. One and a half years later, they tried a second campaign, but were not able to repeat their success. Jasper Versteege admits, "The second time around, we had less preparation and focus. In our first campaign, we were well-prepared and we took our time to do a really good job. In our second campaign, the business was running out of money, and we were trying to launch a spin-off of our crowd lottery concept at the same time. This meant my full attention couldn't be on the campaign, out of necessity. We couldn't delay the campaign because the need for money was urgent. We couldn't delay the other product launch either. Everything had to happen within three months, or the business wouldn't go on. The result was I couldn't give the campaign the attention it needed."

As a result of the failed campaign, Winner Takes All ran out of money and went out of business. Jasper Versteege recalls, "I had to tell all the shareholders from the first offer that it was over, and that their money was gone. It was hard, but I was always clear about the risks. But I am not done. I am already investigating how to re-enter the market."

A failed campaign is feedback. Maybe the timing isn't right, or the presentation is off. But never give up on your dreams.

Hopefully though, you won't find yourself in this position.

You have heard from many startups and growing companies who have done equity crowdfunding, and you now have the tools to follow in their footsteps.

As Alicja Chelbna of Naturalbox says: "It really is possible! Ordinary people are interested in becoming investors in startups, and they actually will engage. I would strongly recommend startups to invite the crowd to become engaged investors. Now everyone has the chance to become a seed investor! We got investors from all over the world; South East Asia, Australia, Singapore, Canada and Dubai. This is so awesome! We now have a global network – imagine that a local company can now go global with the help of equity crowdfunding."

Conclusion

---〜---

"Technology does not wait for us to catch up. From threshing machines and power looms to electricity and assembly lines, to mainframe computers and email, individuals and governments who haven't paid significant attention to new technologies have been in for a nasty shock."

- P. Vigna & M. J. Casey, authors of The Age of Cryptocurrency

Why Equity Crowdfunding Matters

It is a cliché to say that the world is changing fast – people have been saying this for at least the last 150 years and probably longer. But with drones, blockchain technology, self-driving cars, 3-D printing, hover-boards, and the sharing economy either here or close on the horizon, people can sense that this time, it really is different.

With this step-change in entrepreneurship so obviously visible, it is quite striking that most people have barely changed the way they are allocating their investment dollars. We still pump billions of dollars into portfolios made up, largely, of the debt and equity of large corporations, or keep it locked away in the bank at near-zero interest rates.

If the wisdom of stock ownership is ever questioned, fund managers will invariably trot out a well-rehearsed line, saying: *'over the long-run, stock market investments have performed well'*. This will be accompanied by a chart of the historical performance of different asset prices to back up their claim.

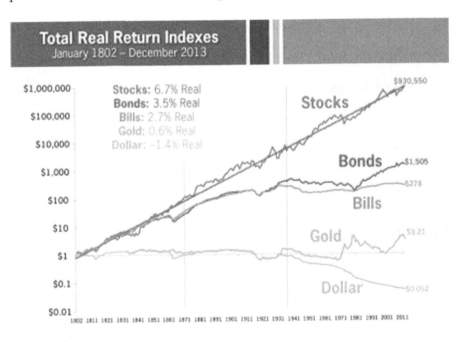

But when it comes to investing, we should not care about the *past*, we should care about the *future* – and the past and the future are *not the same thing*.

Nassim Taleb brought this into sharp focus with his seminal book, _The Black Swan_. The title of Taleb's book comes from the belief of pre-colonial Europeans that all swans were white – a belief which was shattered when Australia was discovered. To their surprise, the early explorers found black swans in this new land, instantly forcing a revision of belief despite the prior data of centuries. No matter how many white swans we see, we cannot definitively say 'all swans are white.' And just because we have over 100 years of backward-looking data saying 'over the long-run, stock market investments have performed well' does not mean we can declare with confidence that stocks are still going to be a good bet for the future.

In the book _Thinking Fast and Slow_, author Daniel Kahneman blames a form of mental laziness called the "affect heuristic" on our tendency to extrapolate the past into the future. The question _'Which assets will outperform in the future'_ is more difficult to answer than _'which assets have outperformed in the past.'_ Our brains, finding the first question to be too tough, will _substitute the second answer for the first question_ – often without us even being conscious of it.

Why has stock ownership performed so well throughout the 20th century, and what evidence suggests that this good run may be coming to an end?

Ron Davison's book _The Fourth Economy_ conceptualizes Western economic growth over the last 700 years. He argues our economic progress has been defined by three distinct stages up to around the year 2000. We had a land-based economy until 1700, where the powerful were the kings and lords who could raise armies and acquire territory. Next, when the industrial revolution took hold, capital became the most important factor for growth, making the banks that controlled it extremely wealthy. Then, around the year 1900, capital became easier to access and the knowledge-based economy of the 20th century took its place, meaning a shortage of educated workers who could plug into corporations. Davison then shows a new, 'fourth economy' is taking shape - which he calls the *entrepreneurial economy*.

The 20th century was exceptionally kind to big corporations. Company laws changed in all kinds of favorable ways. Corporations were able to benefit from globalization to expand their reach, and the bigger they got, the more powerful they became. We had Standard Oil, General Motors, US Steel. Economies of scale ruled the day.

Investing in the stock market generally means investing in large corporations. In most cases, fund managers simply do not have the mandate to invest in small, non-listed companies.

I make the case that owning shares in the stock market (and therefore in large corporations) during the 20th century can be readily compared to owning land during the renaissance, owning capital during the industrial revolution... or owning information, big data, and web traffic today. Therefore, the returns we saw to corporate equity in the 20th century are unlikely to be repeated in the 21st.

We now sit at another transition point. The advantages that corporations once enjoyed are now being dissipated among many more entrepreneurs, targeting many more niches, with very low startup costs breaking down the barriers to entry. As Silicon Valley's Paul Graham put it, "innovation has become more important than scale". We don't need to look far to see proof — these days, small disruptors routinely beat huge incumbents if they have a better idea and better execution.

The question therefore becomes: *during this time of unprecedented disruption, should we be investing in the disruptors, or in the incumbents?*

Thanks to Taleb, the term "Black Swan" has come to be synonymous with high impact, seemingly low probability events – the collapse of communism, September 11, and the credit crunch of 2008/09 being examples. Taleb also convincingly argues that our psychology systematically underestimates the probability of Black Swans, and therefore in financial markets, systematically underprices them.

Equity crowdfunding with potential big winners gives exposure to positive Black Swans. They are investments with capped downside and virtually unlimited upside. People can invest in the growing companies with huge ambitions that need money to bring their plans to fruition.

Equity crowdfunding matters to society because it is helping to fund an economy which is itself in desperate need of renewal. And, ordinary investors gain the ability to participate fully in the new, entrepreneurial economy in this age of disruption.

Parting Thoughts From The Experts

The aim of this book was to be an honest account of equity crowdfunding, and the strategies that work – as testified by the 20 startups and growing companies that have shared their experiences throughout these pages.

On the positive side, equity crowdfunding can really be transformational, and it's not just over-optimistic buzz to say so. Many of the companies I spoke to gushed about the very real surge their businesses had as a result. Several were of the opinion that the exposure they got was even more valuable than the money they raised.

Balancing that, every campaign emphasized the amount of work involved. Also, some felt disappointed that they needed to effectively bring their own investors to their crowdfunding platform, when they were expecting the platform to provide them with a fresh investor audience.

So to conclude, I will leave you with a flavor of the kinds of emotions that could be in front of you, if you decide to go through with a campaign of your own.

Here are a few more thoughts from our experts: the startups and growing companies whose footsteps you could be following in.

~~~

"Our alternatives were banks, angels, and venture capital. We decided on equity crowdfunding because since we are in the business of electric vehicles, we had a good hunch the public would be enthusiastic about our mission. As well as the money, we expected to get some free media time in TV, newspaper and radio, and tie our existing users closer to us. And that's exactly what happened. We have been really pleased with how it turned out."

– Juha Suojanen, EkoRent, raised €171,000 on Invesdor (Finland-headquartered platform).

"Almost all of the money came from persistence and personal emailing from me. I did about six months of non-stop work on our various documents to get the raise ready. It really is an enormous amount of work, and it is very expensive. You need to pay accountants, designers, and possibly legal people as well. It is also extremely stressful."

– Tom Hodgkinson, Idler Academy, raised £149,000 on Crowdcube (UK-headquartered platform).

"The publicity of the offer for us was great. And effectively it was free publicity. There's not that many companies going on these crowdfunding platforms, and they have a lot of people looking at them. We were exposed to a network of several hundred thousand people, and that was invaluable."

– Mark Hughes, Tutora, raised £150,000 on Crowdcube (UK-headquartered platform).

"For us, equity crowdfunding wasn't a way to reach a new crowd. It was a way to raise money from a crowd that we already had."

– Charlie Thuillier, Oppo Ice Cream, raised £650,000 on Seedrs (UK-headquartered platform).

"The overall impact on our business has been incredible. We got great press coverage, and a huge number of new people have heard of us as a result of crowdfunding. I just wish we had raised more!"

– André Moll, MyCouchbox, raised €300,000 on Companisto (Germany-headquartered platform).

"We needed the money, so of course equity crowdfunding has made a huge difference. It allowed us to finish our product development and keep our business growing."

– Ardo Kaurit, Ampler Bikes, raised €91,500 on Fundwise (Estonia-headquartered platform).

"When you end up with 50 or 100 small investors at between $2,000 and $5,000 each, you put in a lot of energy to attract those. And then you have the responsibility to manage them appropriately. Whereas if you had two large cornerstone investors at $250,000 each, you have got a lot less to manage going forward, and maybe you have got people more vested in the outcome."

– Nathan Lawrence, Heyrex, raised NZ$816,000 on Snowball Effect (New Zealand-headquartered platform).

"Before we did our campaign, we looked at another drinks company who were doing crowdfunding. All you see is their page with a few words and a little video, and the money just pouring in. What you don't realize is all the work that has been done to get them to that point."

- Thomas Adner, Caliente, raised €524,000 on FundedByMe (Sweden-headquartered platform).

"The majority of our raise came through existing customers and shareholders. The lesson I learned through the process is that you really need to own the marketing and push it hard."

– Jamie Cairns, CropLogic, raised NZ$512,000 on Equitise (Australia-headquartered platform).

"Once we reached 85%, it went really fast. A lot of people wait until they can see the offer is almost done, before they participate. The last one or two days also went really fast, but that boost in the final days wouldn't have happened if we hadn't got close to our target."

– Eric van Velzen, Nebu, raised €175,000 on Symbid (Netherlands-headquartered platform).

"Crowdfunding gives you great marketing in my opinion. And then there is the access to many great entrepreneurs and business people with experience, who give a new approach to your business."

– Alicja Chlebna, Naturalbox, raised €212,000 on FundedByMe (Sweden-headquartered platform).

"We didn't really build our crowd through crowdfunding. We already had built our crowd, so crowdfunding was simply an opportunity to deepen that relationship."

– Tom Blomfield, Monzo, raised £1 million on Crowdcube (UK-headquartered platform).

"During the life of the campaign, we responded to over 500 requests for information. Many seasoned investors, and many novice investors only interested in putting in £10 or £20."

– Crispin Reeves, Haughton Honey, raised £111,000 on Crowdcube (UK-headquartered platform).

"The biggest challenge was getting traction out of the gate. We didn't want to start with 0% on the slider bar, so we got to 15% when our campaign went live. But once we hit our minimum, we quickly doubled the amount committed in the final week."

– Skai Dalziel, Guusto, raised CA$50,000 on FrontFundr (Canada-headquartered platform).

"Equity crowdfunding is like running fifteen marathons."

– Jarno Alastalo, Heimo, raised €170,000 on Invesdor (Finland-headquartered platform).

"The entire process, from deciding to go down the crowdfunding route to having the cash in our bank account took five months. Three of those months were very full-on."

– Alex Zivoder, goHenry, raised £3.99 million on Crowdcube (UK-headquartered platform).

"Doing a full-fledged campaign requires your full focus. You just can't do it on the side when you've got too many other big things going on in your business. People won't just come to you and find you unless you prepare it well."

– Jasper Versteege, Winner Takes All, raised €80,000 on FundedByMe (Sweden-headquartered platform).

"Time-wise, it took one of our company directors about one month, full-time. Public relations and legal costs added up to around NZ$15,000."

– Tom Mayo, SOS, raised NZ$252,000 on Snowball Effect (New Zealand-headquartered platform).

"We spent two years of work building our community, and to get the media explaining how our technology works and why we do what we do. I do a lot of events and conferences and meet a lot of people. That's why we were successful."

– Sandra Rey, Glowee, raised €611,000 on WiSEED (France-headquartered platform).

"The way we looked at it, raising the money privately might have been cheaper and faster, but crowdfunding just had so many other upsides – in better investment terms, and better publicity, that for us it just made total sense."

– Laurence Cook, Pavegen, raised £1.90 million on Crowdcube (UK-headquartered platform).

Among such a diverse group of company founders, such a varied range of experiences should not come as a surprise.

Even so, common themes have clearly emerged. The technological and legal changes underpinning equity crowdfunding may have enabled a new way of raising capital, but the fundamental rules of investing have not changed. You still need to have a worthy business if you want to get funded. Attracting investors still takes work. Launching with momentum is absolutely fundamental to your chances. And to use the real power of the crowd, you need to stay engaged with your new investors long after your offer has ended.

I am personally very excited about the potential for equity crowdfunding, and I hope you are too. When we encourage people to explore direct ownership in private companies, we will get citizens with greater levels of financial education, taking responsibility for themselves and their futures. It will also supercharge the entrepreneurial economy.

Equity crowdfunding is part of a larger cultural change towards a more open, more technologically-based, more decentralized economy. It gives worthy companies the access to investors who want to back them of their own free will. It will forge more direct relationships between companies and the people that surround them – their crowd. This will irrevocably change the culture of investing.

If you feel inspired to join the equity crowdfunding revolution, I wish you many happy returns.

At this point, you will want to know the next steps.

How can you find an equity crowdfunding platform to approach? There were a lot of platforms mentioned in this book, and you need to know where they are based, and how to contact them.

You might also want to check out some of the campaign pages of the featured companies to see how they presented themselves.

I have organized all of this for you. Download the directory of the 20 startups and growing companies, the 12 equity crowdfunding platforms, and all the experts who contributed to this book at **www.nathanrose.me/equity**.

One Last Thing

If you found value in this book, I would hugely appreciate it if you would take a few seconds and go to **amazon.com** and leave a review. It will help spread the message to other startups and growing companies.

Any business that wants to raise money and promote themselves at the same time will be grateful for the recommendation. Remember, without reviews, you probably would never have found this book.

Here's how:

- Go to **amazon.com** and find the book. (Easiest is to type "Equity Crowdfunding" into the search bar.)
- Once you are on the book's Amazon page, scroll down to the part that says: "Customer Reviews". It looks like this:

Customer Reviews

☆☆☆☆☆ 50
4.9 out of 5 stars ▾

5 star		94%
4 star		6%
3 star		0%
2 star		0%
1 star		0%

Share your thoughts with other customers

Write a customer review

See all 50 customer reviews ›

- Click the button that says "Write a customer review". It is the button the arrow is pointing to in the above screenshot.
- Give it a rating (out of FIVE STARS), and write a short sentence of recommendation.

Please take just 30 seconds of your time to support an independent author by leaving a rating. Thank you so much!

Nathan Rose
www.nathanrose.me
contact@nathanrose.me

Sample Chapter:
Rewards Crowdfunding

———— ～ ————

This is a sample of one of my other books.

Rewards crowdfunding can be used to validate project ideas, build an audience, and raise the necessary cash to get it off the ground. Rewards Crowdfunding is the step-by-step playbook for creators intending to launch a campaign of their own. Learn the best strategies from two dozen successful creators, and the world's leading crowdfunding launch agencies.

For information on how to order, go to:
www.nathanrose.me/rewards

———— ～ ————

What Is Rewards Crowdfunding?

Crowdfunding refers to the practice of using the Internet to solicit money from a large number of people. Small individual contributions aggregate into a significant sum when enough people contribute.

It is an alternative to seeking funding from a single entity, such as a bank. From the creator's point of view, the problem with banks and other institutional sources of finance is that it places too much power in the hands of just one party. The entity with the money has all the power to decide which projects they fund and which they do not.

Crowdfunding means creators get to set their own terms and let the crowd decide whether their project is worthy. It means it doesn't matter as much if one person says 'no'. Crowdfunding is about how an audience *as a whole* responds - just as a performer on stage can still receive a raucous applause, even if some people in the crowd choose not to clap.

The crowdfunding phenomenon is broader than the subject of this book. The differences between the various types of crowdfunding lie in the type of project being funded, and what is being promised to those that contribute the cash.

- **Equity Crowdfunding:** people get shares of ownership in the company raising funds, thereby becoming investors

- **Debt Crowdfunding:** people become lenders, expecting the borrower to repay the money later (often with interest)

- **Real Estate Crowdfunding:** people become partial-owners of real-estate properties

- **Donation Crowdfunding:** people give the money as charity, with no expectation of getting anything in return

- **Rewards Crowdfunding:** people are promised a product or other perks in exchange for their pledge

Equity crowdfunding, debt crowdfunding, and real estate crowdfunding are all investments. The investors stand to profit if the crowdfunded venture performs well. Meanwhile, donation crowdfunding is gifted to help those in need - for example, funding a medical procedure, paying for education, or for humanitarian relief efforts.

Rewards crowdfunding backers are not expecting financial returns, but it is not a something-for-nothing proposition either. Instead, backers are promised a physical item, a digital download, an experience, or something else of value. It may be helpful to think of pledging to a rewards crowdfunding campaign as being similar to pre-ordering a product. The creator gets the cash first, and then uses it to create and deliver something to their backers.

Helping creative projects get off the ground is the strongest use case for rewards crowdfunding. There should be something new and different about the project. In order to take full advantage of the global reach of the Internet, ideally the perks should be capable of being delivered to far-away locations.

In summary, rewards crowdfunding has four main elements:

1. Using the Internet…

2. …to raise money from a large number of small backers…

3. …for creative projects…

4. …by promising perks to those backers

How Does It Work?

So, rewards crowdfunding sees people go online to pledge money towards creative projects in return for perks to be delivered at a future date. But how does that happen exactly?

Here are some key terms to become familiar with:

- **Platforms**: The websites which host campaigns for potential backers to view. There are multiple campaigns running on each platform.

- **Campaigns**: Conducted by the creators attempting to raise money. Campaigns use platforms to publish their pitch where they explain their project and try to convince backers to pledge their financial support.

- **Backers**: The individuals who pledge money towards campaigns, and expect to receive perks in return. Backers discover campaigns by visiting platforms.

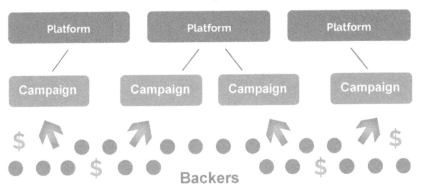

HOW REWARDS CROWDFUNDING WORKS

Platforms host campaigns which backers can decide whether to pledge money to

If you have never seen a rewards crowdfunding platform before, it is worth checking one out. Visit Kickstarter or Indiegogo (which are, by far, the world's two largest rewards crowdfunding platforms at the time of writing), and navigate to find a campaign. Each individual campaign page has information about their project. You may see a video, written information, images, animations, and written text explaining what they are hoping to accomplish. Visitors can also ask questions and receive answers from the creator behind the campaign. Finally, there is a place where visitors can click to pledge money.

Campaigns need to decide on a **funding goal**, which is the target amount they are seeking to raise. Some platforms mandate all campaigns must have a 'fixed funding goal', in which case this becomes the minimum amount of money necessary for the campaign to be successful. For example, if a campaign were to set a fixed funding goal of $10,000, but only $7,000 was pledged, then the campaign would fail and the creator would get nothing (not even the $7,000). Other crowdfunding platforms allow the option of a 'flexible funding goal', where campaigns can keep whatever money they raise, regardless of whether they make it to their stated funding goal or not.

Campaigns must also set a **deadline**, which is the final date where the campaign closes and cannot accept any more money.

Each campaign usually offers several **reward tiers** (or **perks**, which is a different word for the same thing). Generally, the more money a backer pledges, the more generous the promised rewards / perks. These tiers can also be used to motivate urgent action - for example, by creating exclusive early bird offers only available to backers who commit quickly.

Campaigns also need to decide upon a **delivery date** for the rewards they promise. If the campaign is successful, it is up to the creator to deliver the rewards to their backers within this timeframe. It is quite common for the delivery date to be several months after the end of the campaign, or sometimes even longer.

Below is a screenshot from a campaign for 'Sherlock Holmes Hexalogy', by Thornwillow Press. It successfully raised US$92,322 from 421 *backers* on Kickstarter, having exceeded its *funding goal* of US$6,000 by the *deadline* of July 11, 2017. Two of the *reward tiers* are visible in this screenshot - a US$60 pledge would see backers promised a paper-wrapper bound version of the book, and a US$120 pledge would land them a cloth-binding edition. They promised a *delivery date* of October 2017, around 3 months after the end of the campaign.

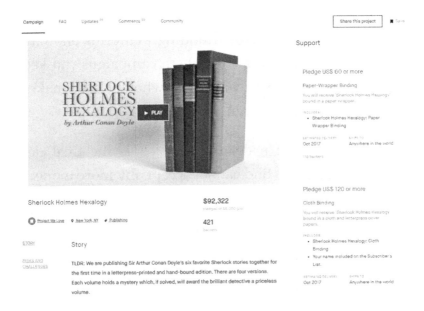

Backer Motivations

When you think about it, backers are doing something rather unusual - particularly in today's age of instant gratification and overnight shipping. Outside of rewards crowdfunding, products get delivered to customers fairly quickly - within days, or maybe weeks at most. But rewards crowdfunding backers very often don't get their items until many *months* have passed. Why are backers prepared to wait such a long time?

You should understand the motivations of rewards crowdfunding backers. Some of these motivations will be more relevant to your campaign than others. Your messaging will depend on which of them you decide to primarily target.

Motivation #1: To Get It First

Works Best For - Highly Innovative Technology Products

Mark Pecota is the CEO of LaunchBoom, and he shares his perspective on this backer motivation: "There are always going to be some people who want to have the latest and greatest products in their hands before anyone else. We call them 'innovators' and 'early adopters', and rewards crowdfunding caters very well to them."

This is especially true of technology products. Die-hard fans will camp overnight outside Apple stores, so they can be among the first to get the newest iPhone as soon as it is released. In the same vein, offering backers first access to your product can be very compelling.

If you promise early access, make sure that you mean it! Backers become very annoyed if they see the item for sale elsewhere, before they have received it themselves.

Motivation #2: To Get An Exclusive

Works Best For - Artistic Projects (Documentaries, Books, Music)

Depending on the project, it may be possible to offer customization, or versions which will only be available to crowdfunding backers (and not afterward). Examples include having the backer's name engraved on the product, or to make it in a color of the backer's choosing.

However, a word of warning: many creators lamented the customization they promised during the campaign as being a real pain to ultimately deliver once the campaign was over. Worst of all was when more than one item of customization was on offer in a single reward tier.

Artistic projects are especially well-placed to take advantage of this backer motivation through offering exclusive access to the creator. Roger Sherman (a co-founder of Florentine Films) is the producer, director, cinematographer, photographer, author, and documentary doctor behind 'In Search of Israeli Cuisine' - a portrait of the Israeli people, told through food. Sherman received a US$10,000 pledge from a single backer by offering an Associate Producer credit on the film roll and the chance to accompany him on a post-production session. This reward cost Sherman barely anything to fulfill, apart from a little of his time.

Motivation #3: To Support A Cause

Works Best For - Community / Friends-And-Family Campaigns

The line between rewards crowdfunding and donation crowdfunding can become blurred. Not all rewards crowdfunding backers are asking: *'what's in it for me?'*. Backers may also support a cause if it is near and dear to their hearts. This can be particularly powerful for campaigns with a social impact or sustainability angle. These backers may be spurred into action by understanding: *'If I don't back this campaign, then it will not happen.'*

If friends and family are asked to pledge, then the creator may *themselves* be the 'cause' that is being supported. If backers know the creator personally, then they might back the campaign because they want to see the creator follow their passion project. Creators may even be able to reach their funding goal purely through friends and family, if the funding goal is not too high.

However, your immediate circle is unlikely to be enough for campaigns aiming to raise larger amounts - say over US$25,000 - unless you are connected to a *lot* of very generous people! Campaigns with greater ambitions will need to position themselves to attract the attention of strangers. Also, relying on friends and family is something of a one-time tactic - people may be happy to help the first time, but creators shouldn't go cap-in-hand to friends and family repeatedly for their second, third, and subsequent crowdfunding campaigns.

Motivation #4: To Find Community

Works Best For - Board Games

People form tribes around brands and products which foster a shared experience. This backer motivation is strongest in crowdfunded board games. Backers enjoy having a say in how the game turns out, telling their friends they had a part in creating it, and then play together with them.

Ben Hoban raised AU$144,980 on Kickstarter for 'The Brigade', a fantasy firefighting board game. He saw first-hand how a vibrant community developed during his campaign: " People weren't buying the game as much as they were buying into that experience of being with other people on the comments board. They wanted to talk about it, and be part of the instant community that sprang up. As a creator, that can be intoxicating - people are coming together and rallying around your idea."

Motivation #5: To Get It Cheaper

Works Best For - Consumer Items, Impulse Purchases

Creators can offer perks at a discount from the price they will be sold at post-campaign. The discount needs to be *generous*, especially if backers are being asked to wait a long time for delivery. Generally speaking, a 10% discount would be viewed as too insignificant, whereas discounts of at least 30% are more likely to convince people to back the crowdfunding campaign.

Tom Hannaher raised US$33,541 on Kickstarter for 'ZVOX Noise Canceling Headphones'. This campaign offered a discount of around 40% off the eventual retail price. The headphones were essentially production-ready at the time of the campaign, so their message was mostly about backers getting the best possible deal.

Hannaher explains their strategy: "ZVOX is an established company. We don't really need money to fund our product development. We start our crowdfunding campaigns when our production schedule is firmly known - sometimes even when production has already begun! For us, crowdfunding is an excellent marketing tool to expose our brand to a tech-savvy group of people. It's a great way for us to introduce a product. We can quickly establish a customer base by selling hundreds of units before we have announced it to the general public."

ZVOX delivered the headphones within weeks of their campaign conclusion, which is much faster than most crowdfunding campaigns. For their backers, it resembled ordering ready-to-deliver goods. Rewards crowdfunding fits well for ZVOX because it helps get early customer reviews and testimonials, which then become useful for selling through their other channels.

Co-Creation vs. Features-And-Benefits

In addition to the above five backer motivations, another useful model classifies backers into just two varieties:

- **Co-creators** are interested in the campaign back-story and mission. These backers want to be part of the creative journey, providing their feedback along the way.

- **Customers** just want the rewards the campaign offers. These backers prefer to have a transactional experience, similar to what they normally get when ordering products.

Some argue that the true 'spirit' of rewards crowdfunding is about co-creators, not customers. Co-creators are more *in love* with the project than customers are. Co-creators are also more willing to go out of their way to help the campaign succeed, and are more forgiving of mistakes.

But the co-creator relationship takes time and effort to develop. Just like romantic human love, cultivating a deep bond does not happen overnight. Because of this, some creators deliberately choose to make a product-based pitch rather than an emotional one. Campaigns can still do very well with this strategy - after all, this is how most products are sold to customers outside of rewards crowdfunding.

Targeting either co-creators or customers can work, but you need to decide which type of backer you primarily want to get on board. There will probably be one kind of message you are more comfortable conveying. **Co-creation campaigns** go with more emotive storytelling, while **features-and-benefits campaigns** focus more singularly on the product.

Campaigns are never entirely one or the other. Even a mostly co-creation campaign needs to include the features-and-benefits of the rewards on offer, and vice-versa. Still, most campaigns have a bias towards one side. The distinction between 'co-creation campaigns' vs. 'features-and-benefits campaigns' will be highlighted throughout the book whenever it is important.

You now know what rewards crowdfunding is and how it works. Creators can use it to raise money for their project through a limited-time campaign hosted on an online platform. They set a funding target, which if reached, results in the creator being obliged to deliver perks to their backers by a certain date. There are many ways creators can make their project appealing, so long as the backer motivations are kept front-of-mind.

With these basics handled, the next chapter moves to how this applies to the project you have in mind. Let's evaluate whether rewards crowdfunding is the best choice for you and your idea.

Enjoyed reading this sample?

Want to read the rest?

For information on how to order, go to:

www.nathanrose.me/rewards

Acknowledgments

The idea for this book came during a month spent with other location-independent entrepreneurs organized by Chris Reynolds. The time there inspired me, and introduced me to some amazing people, many of whom have gone on to become great friends.

To achieve anything requires both inspiration and perspiration. With the inspiration part handled by the Entrepreneur House, I credit the perspiration to Tal Gur. He has been with me on this journey over the last 9 months as my coach, friend, and sparring partner at chess! When we speak every two weeks I can throw just about any question or problem at him, and he will invariably have an actionable answer. It is staggering how one man could know so much about so many different things. Thanks Tal for your patience and wisdom. It may sound trite to say "it wouldn't have happened without you," but without Tal, this book really would not have.

As a first-time author, I was very lucky to be able to draw upon the advice of some very smart people who had published books of their own previously: Esther Jacobs, Gregory Diehl, Peter Shankman, and Rob Dix gave me the inside word on how to write and promote a book. Additionally, Scott Cardwell and Eli David are a couple of marketing mavens who provided very useful ideas.

The startups and growing companies that featured in this book shared the advice that formed the book's most valuable content. Juha Suojanen, Tom Hodgkinson, Charlie Thuillier, André Moll, Ardo Kaurit, Mark Hughes, Nathan Lawrence, Thomas Adner, Jamie Cairns, Eric van Velzen, Alicja Chlebna, Tom Blomfield, Crispin Reeves, Skai Dalziel, Jarno Alastalo, Alex Zivoder, Jasper Versteege, Laurence Cook, Tom Mayo, and Sandra Rey have not only my thanks for sharing what they learned, but also my admiration for pulling off their successful campaigns.

Without the leaders who have guided the industry through these formative years, the entire subject of this book would not exist. Ronald Kleverlaan deserves a special mention for writing a foreword that I was honored by, and for hosting me for a month in Amsterdam at CrowdfundingHub. Crowdfunding experts Sandi Gilbert, Bret Conkin, Anna Hakvoort, Brock Murray, Jaap Dekter, and Andrew Dix all contributed greatly. So did those who are in the driver's seat of the equity crowdfunding platforms: Frank Webster, Luke Lang, Peter Moore, Josh Daniell, Jesper Viveen, Will Mahon-Heap, Tamo Zwinge, Chris Thomas, Kendrick Nguyen, Tom Britton, Sean Burke, and Yannig Roth.

Authors need feedback, and there is no getting around the fact that doing so is time-consuming. When a request lands in your inbox to read a draft of a 50,000-word book, the easiest thing to do is to ignore it – and, given our busy lives, this is a perfectly reasonable response. But some brave souls instead decided to review my typo-laden first draft. They amazed me with the detail and insight they provided in their responses. To Josh Riddiford, Justin Soong, Gary Mersham, Sandy Voigt, Kat

Jenkins, Logan Elliot, Sue Rose, Luke Williams, Robert Huang, Raewyn Bartley, Simon Papa, Ronen Lev, Barry Grehan, Francis Reid, Raul Avina, Max Reinhardt, Luni Libes, Ilya Ochnev, Mark Gardner, and Charles Ehredt – I really do appreciate it, and I owe you one.

Finally, there were others, too numerous to name, who helped me design the cover, decide on a title, and provided encouragement throughout. I'm grateful for all of your contributions.

And of course, there wouldn't be any point at all without the reader. So thanks to you, for reading my book.

Copyright & Disclaimer

Third Edition, 2020

ISBN:

- 978-0-473-37798-4 (Paperback)

- 978-0-473-37799-1 (E-Book)

- 978-0-473-37800-4 (Audio Book)

www.nathanrose.me/equity

Made in the USA
Coppell, TX
04 February 2021